The Energy of Life

A GUIDE TO PRACTICAL SPIRITUALITY

BARBARA & JIMMIE LEWIS

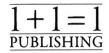

$$\overline{1+1=1}$$
PUBLISHING

1+1=1 Publishing
1344 Jones Street
Sonoma, CA 95476
1plus1publishing@gmail.com

Cover photo, with permission,
is an original painting by
artist Deborah Gall titled "New Life"
www.deborahgall.com

Printed in the United States of America
First Edition: April 1995
Second Printing: April 2002
Second Edition: April 2015
10 9 8 7 6 5 4 3 2 1
ISBN: 978-0-9914629-2-6

DEDICATION

The Energy of Life is dedicated to
the energy that Barbara Lewis was, and is,
and to the voice in which it is written, which is hers.

Barbara Ann Kenney Lewis
May 23, 1953 – August 31, 2010

ACKNOWLEDGEMENTS

*To Michael and Phyllis Lewis Hyland
for their belief in me.*

*To Phyllis Lewis Hyland
for her untiring efforts
on my behalf.*

CONTENTS

PROLOGUE

*Yet what is true in God's creation cannot enter here
until it is reflected in some form the world can understand.*
—A Course in Miracles, Lesson 138

Walking our dog, Max, around the large inner circle of our rural subdivision on the outskirts of New Orleans early one Saturday morning in the very early 1990's, Barbara began receiving Divine inspiration for this book. We just didn't know it was going to be a book at the time.

What Barbara said to me was, "Jimmie, anytime we judge anyone or anything, we separate ourselves from ourselves." It was like an arrow had pierced my closed heart and all of a sudden I felt within my entire being the truth of Barbara's words. I knew they were true. We spent the rest of our walk with a whole litany of ideas pouring out of Barbara's wide-open mind, all of which explained, enhanced, supported and clarified the meaning, and applicability, of Barbara's first sentence about judgment and separation.

We knew shortly thereafter that all of these ideas were going to go into a book, our first, and we worked excitedly and inspired toward that end. The writing, however, except for notes about the writing, was not to come until the end. The work was a several year process of receiving, processing and learning to believe and accept what we were being taught.

We felt like we were being given the blueprint to how the world works and, even more importantly, to how our minds work in relation to the outside world. So we called the book, *The Energy of Life*, referring to the underlying energetic blueprint of how the world does work along with the cause and effect relationship of our mind to the world.

The Energy of Life is written in Barbara's voice, with mine embedded throughout in everything from small nuances to whole paragraphs. In issuing this Second Edition and adding the subtitle, *A Guide to Practical Spirituality*, all that I have done is to add chapter subtitles for emphasis and clarity which is the same purpose of the sub-title, along with this Prologue.

Welcome to the energy of your life. May you master it and learn to create the life you want.

Introduction

— ENERGY BLUEPRINT —

Energy is something we all learned about in school. There was kinetic, thermal, potential and many other different kinds of energy that we studied. But one thing we didn't learn in school is about the energy that exists within and around us, let's call it vibrational energy. We didn't learn that this energy can affect how we think, or react and it can even affect what kinds of people and circumstances we have in our lives.

Learning about this energy within and around you can help you get what you really want out of life. Learning about this energy can be like having a blueprint for creating your very own dream come true. This may sound like a lot of rehashed positive thinking, but it's not. Sometimes, a positive attitude may mask the real energy that a person is putting out and therefore may block them from ever getting what they really want. What we're talking about in this book is changing the energy in and around your life to create the kind of world that you want.

There are those of you who are reading this and feel that the situations and circumstances in your life are totally beyond your control. By reading this book, you will have to challenge those beliefs. You will have to decide if you think that there are some of us in this world who are born "lucky" or if we are all basically born into this world with the same power to change ourselves and our environment. You will have to decide if you think that there is some higher power that grants "good" situations to some and "bad" situations to others or that you help to create everything that is going on around you in this world.

We have spent years watching, experimenting and playing with the energy in our lives. This book is an attempt to document some of what we have learned and to make some of the concepts relating to energy more understandable for everyone. There have been others who have written about these subjects before. We are not claiming to have invented new concepts or universal laws. We are just trying to simplify these concepts by defining and limiting any terminology relating to spirituality or psychology and explain all concepts in very practical ways.

— GET WHAT YOU WANT OUT OF LIFE —

We also don't claim to have all the answers to your life or ours. Life is a learning process for us all and we are not exempt. Certainly we are always growing and changing. That's part of what makes life so exciting. With each new day, there is growth and sometimes change. But over the years we have noticed that there are certain properties of energy that remain constant. By knowing more about these properties of energy, it will help you to get what you want out of life.

What we will share with you is how the energy of desire works, how you attract people and circumstances to your life, and how to read the energy of situations you find yourself in. But the most important thing we will share with you is how to unblock your own pure energy so that you can get what you really want out of life.

— A MIRROR FOR YOU —

One of the most beautiful aspects of our marriage is the gentle way we are able to mirror to one another the kinds of energy we see in each other's life. We have found that as we open up to these lessons and quit resisting, life becomes easier and more peaceful and day by day we get closer to realizing our dreams. Our intent in writing this book is to gently hold up a mirror for you. You can see as much or as little as you want to see in the mirror. We can't, and neither can anyone else, tell you exactly what kind of energy is stored within and around you. But we can promise you this. When you look in the mirror and see the truth about yourself you will recognize it as the truth. Something inside of you will click. There will be a sensation of a big "aha" and you will be able to see thoughts, feelings, beliefs and actions that may have been sabotaging your dreams. The more you open up to the energy inside of you and are willing to take a look at it, the more your life will seem to get easier and you will attract the very things your heart desires.

— HIDING FROM THE TRUTH —

Before we get into talking about energy, let us first tell you a little about what it feels like to be hiding from the truth, for those of you who may be feeling some resistance already. Basically, if you feel any type of negativity to any new idea that you haven't tried out in your life yet, then there's a good chance that somewhere inside of you there is something that you may not want to know about yourself. If this happens, just try to stay open and consider what is being said. You may find that after a few hours, days or months, you are more willing to take a look at the truth.

Reading about new ideas is a lot like clothes shopping. If you will just try them on, you will see which ones fit. Oftentimes, you will miss a great opportunity for growth (or a great outfit!) if you stubbornly refuse to try something new.

Of course, we don't want you to accept at face value anything we say here as law, the truth or as dogma. What will be most beneficial for you is for you to stay open to all ideas and try them out in your life. If they work for you, great! If they don't, great! Move on to what does work for you in your life. We can't urge you strongly enough. Just think for yourself!

ENERGY

In our introduction we have used the word energy many times.
This is because you must first learn about energy
in order to find out how to make your dreams come true.
And to learn more about energy,
you must first open your mind to new possibilities
and new ways of thinking.

— VIBRATING ENERGY —

Western scientists have finally accepted what has been handed down for centuries in the teachings of the Far East. Scientists now agree that everything in the universe is made of the same thing: energy. And they also agree that the energy that everything is made of vibrates. If you break everything down to its smallest unit you will find small particles of vibrating energy. Your clothes, the furniture in your home, your money and your car are all made of the same thing: vibrating energy. What makes one thing different from another is simply the rate at which the energy vibrates within a given object. The energy of your body vibrates at a rate that we see through our eyes as a human body. One article of clothing vibrates at a rate that we see as, perhaps, blue cotton, while another piece of clothing vibrates at another rate that we call gray wool.

This concept is similar to one you already accept. Ice, water and steam are all made of the same thing, molecules of H2O. Yet the rate at which they vibrate is what distinguishes one from the other. If you take all substances in the world down to their smallest unit, what scientists now have discovered is that those units are the same. They are all energy that vibrates at different rates.

You might be skeptical because you can't actually see your clothing vibrate and you can't see any energy vibrating in and around your furniture. But think for a moment of all the things you accept as truth in your life that you can't see. Every day, you plug in your hairdryer or your toaster and although you can't see the electricity or the electric energy, you accept that it is there. In fact, you've probably spent your money on electricity for years and you've never seen it. You've only seen its effects.

When you are out on the beach, you accept that the ultraviolet rays of the sun can burn your skin, but you can't really see these rays or their energy. Again, you can only see and sometimes feel the effects of the sun's energy. Almost every day of our lives we all watch television or listen to the radio and we just accept that there are television and radio waves of energy that are being broadcast to our receivers, even though we can't see these waves. But we can see or hear their effects.

The point is that there are many things that we can't sense with our five senses and yet we still believe in them. We have only named a few here, but you can probably think of others. We believe in them because we can see, hear, taste or feel their effects. In the same way, the vibrational energy in your life is not something you can see, hear, taste, or touch.

However, if you know how to look for the effects of vibrational energy, you can easily find them.

— ENERGY SOURCE —

So where does all of this vibrating energy comes from? A word of caution here; you may bump into your religious beliefs during this discussion, but this is not about religion, although it is in the genre of spirituality.

If everything is made of the same thing, vibrating energy, where did it come from? Many of you will say God. Some of you will say you don't know. And there are a lot of you with theories in between. Most of us, however, have some kind of belief or idea that everything comes from some tremendously powerful energy source. Whether you label it as God or use no label at all, most of us have some kind of inner sense that everything comes from the same wonderful, powerful energy source.

Stop for a moment if you will. Think about what we've just said here. Everything, absolutely everything, comes from the same magnificent energy source. Most of us never take the time to think about this, but where else could everything come from? Think about the energy source that makes the tides of the oceans ebb and flow, always perfectly, always in balance. Think about the energy source that causes an embryo to form and to eventually turn out to be a baby with incredible bodily functions that marvel even the most intelligent of minds. That same energy source that makes all of nature work, that causes your heart to pump and your lungs to breathe has created everything in the universe: everything, including you.

Take a few minutes to close your eyes and imagine where you came from. Don't think about this in the sense of coming from your mom and dad. Think about the way some magnificent energy source extended itself into your mother's womb and created you out of its own energy. If you get nothing else from this book, get this. You came from a wondrous energy source. You are the same energy as the magnificent energy source that created and now runs the universe. And so is every other human being. And so is every living thing. And so is everything in the entire universe.

— UNIQUE EXPRESSION —

The question arises, then, that since we are all made of the same energy, does this mean we are not unique? Quite the contrary, each of us is a unique expression of this same wondrous energy source. Some of us have blond hair, some brown skin, some of us are considered tall, some of us have an overt sexual quality, and others have aggressive, powerful personalities. There is an infinite number of physical, mental and spiritual expressions and no two are the same. Even in the case of identical twins, each is a unique expression of the same energy source.

Each of these infinite expressions of the wondrous energy source is a correct, right and perfect expression. It is only in our society that we label and judge some expressions to be undesirable, ugly or bad. What's always been puzzling to us is how we, as human beings, seem to celebrate the diversity of nature except when it comes to our own species. We build zoos and aquariums to be able to admire the different kinds of animal life. And we create botanical gardens to celebrate the different kinds of plant life. Many of us spend countless hours in volunteer work to preserve certain species of animal life or woods or wetlands. Many of us also build our leisure time around activities that celebrate the diversity of nature. We snorkel, scuba, bird watch, plant flower gardens or go on safari.

So why is it that when we get to our own species we want us all to look, think and act alike? Why don't we celebrate when we meet someone who is different than ourselves? We delight in the discovery of animals and plants that have different expressions. Why isn't it a delightful discovery for us every time we meet another human being who is different than ourselves? It could be a wonderful adventure for us to discover the unique ways that the same energy source that created us also created a different expression in a like species. It could also be a pleasure for us just to express ourselves in our own natural way instead of constantly trying to edit ourselves to be like everyone else. But for most of us, it isn't like that, is it? Why is that?

If you asked most people that same question of why we, as a society, don't admire and appreciate the differences in our own species, you'd probably get answers like "fear of the unknown", "not understanding people who are different" or maybe "I just can't relate". And if you asked those same people why they go through contortions trying to "fit in" instead of just going with their natural tendencies, you'd probably get answers like "I just want to be normal" or "I don't want to stick out". But it goes much deeper than that.

— CONSCIOUSNESS —

To begin to answer these questions, we must first talk about consciousness. Webster's New World Dictionary defines the word consciousness as the totality of one's thoughts, feelings and impressions. When you were born, your consciousness was like the pure, wonderful energy source that created you. Why do you think babies cause so many people to feel so much love inside? Perhaps they serve as a reminder to us of the pure energy that we started with, the pure consciousness of the wonderful energy source that created us. Maybe, when you pick up a baby, the baby's pure vibrating energy connects with that same pure vibrating energy deep inside of you and reminds you of who you really are.

So, if we all started with this wonderful, pure, radiant consciousness, what happened to it along the way? As you experienced life, you began to experience the energy of other's beliefs, thoughts, feelings and actions and you began to mix their energy in with yours and cover up your natural energy. You started piling the energy of false beliefs in on top of the pure, wondrous energy that you are made of. And that became your consciousness, your own unique version of energy that vibrates inside and around you. So, at any given moment of your life, your consciousness is a combination of the pure, wondrous life energy you started with and the energy of all of the beliefs, thoughts, feelings and impressions that you allowed and are still allowing to mix in with it.

— ICEBERG —

There is another thing you should know about your consciousness. You may not be consciously aware of what is in it. Here we'd like to use an analogy that many of you may have heard in a self-help context. Your consciousness is like an iceberg. Part of it is the conscious part, or the part of the iceberg that you can actually see.

The other part (which is much larger) is the unconscious part, or the part of the iceberg that you can't see. So you may think your consciousness has certain kinds of thoughts, beliefs, feelings or impressions in it, when in reality, it might have just the opposite kinds of thoughts, beliefs, feelings or impressions in it. You may think your energy is like the pure wondrous energy you started life with, but unbeknownst to you is the fact that you mixed in the energy of a lot of false beliefs. The sad part is that just like a ship can get wrecked by the part of an iceberg that is hidden, so can your life and dreams get sabotaged by the hidden energy within and around you.

Most of us have taken on the energy of so many false beliefs that we have actually forgotten about our pure, core energy. We have forgotten who we really are. When we look inside, all we see is the energy of the false beliefs. When some of us look inside, all we see is ugliness, separation, pain, or maybe self-loathing. And sometimes, looking at that energy deep inside us is so ugly, scary or painful that we would rather do literally anything than look at it. Many of us are addicted to very destructive patterns in our lives, but we continue because the patterns of addiction anesthetize or distract us from the fear or pain of looking at ourselves. We hide out in drugs, alcohol, work, religion, food, judgment of others, love relationships, sex, you name it! We find lots of ways to distract and/or anesthetize ourselves. And what we're really afraid of, what we're really avoiding, is looking at who we are inside.

Still others of us prevent ourselves from really taking a look inside by repeatedly excusing ourselves. Before we have a chance to rationally look at an issue in our lives, we say things to ourselves like, "It was the best I could do for where I was at the time." Although self-acceptance and non-judgment are good and healthy choices, taken to the extreme, they can be good places to hide out from ourselves.

— DENIAL —

One of the most well disguised ways of hiding out and not looking inside yourself is denial. Many people claim to have no friction in their lives and no problems to deal with. From the outside, it looks as if they are living perfect storybook lives and everything they do revolves around the promotion of that facade. These are the people who "have it all wired" and insist on being right. To this type of person, an admission that they have any real type of problem is the same as saying that there is something wrong with them, which, to them, is an unbearable thought. These people have really forgotten about their magnificent, unlimited core energy and live their lives based on a fragile belief system of perfection. And since we are all basically imperfect human beings or we wouldn't be here, this type of person will always have a friction or pain inside of them. They will also be terrified of letting go of their perfection facade and looking at their real selves.

— CORE ENERGY —

But whatever your mode of hiding out from the real you deep inside of yourself, try to get past it if you can. If you could remember the moment that you were created you wouldn't be so scared. If you could remember that at the core of every cell in your body, your spirit and your mind is the same wondrous energy that created everything in the universe, perhaps it wouldn't be such a scary thing to take a look at yourself. Inside of all of us exists a very pure, beautiful, loving energy. At our core, we are all made up of the same beautiful energy. No matter how many false beliefs have been added, it's still down there. So try to wade through your fears about examining your own energy and looking at your consciousness, both the conscious and unconscious parts. In the end, if you continue in your journey of awareness, you will meet up with the magnificent, wondrous energy at your core. At your core, you will meet up with an energy of abundance, fullness, beauty, health, freedom, power, excellence, fulfillment, unlimitedness, intelligence and harmony.

— FALSE BELIEFS —

Let us give you some examples of how false beliefs can get mixed in with your pure, core energy and change your consciousness. Let's say you were raised in a family where your parents believed that there was never enough to go around and they passed that belief on to you in their thoughts and actions. You always heard from your parents that "we can't afford that" and "rich people can't be trusted". When your mom cooked for all eight of you, she cooked one chicken and you had to fight with your siblings for enough food to satisfy your hunger. When Christmas came around, charities would come by your house to bring gifts. Otherwise you would have gotten nothing at all.

Now you are an adult and you can't understand why you can't get a good job or why you can't pay your bills. What happened was you mixed your wondrous abundant energy with the false belief of your parents that there is not enough to go around. The energy of their actions and thoughts was about poverty, not abundance. And you took it in. Does that mean your parents did a bad job raising you? Certainly not! They probably did their best and you must remember that they were also raised by human beings who passed along imperfect, false beliefs to them as well. You have to remember that they grew up in an imperfect society that gave them false impressions. The point to realize here is that underneath your false belief of lack still lies your wondrous abundant energy. And getting back to that energy is the key to changing your financial situation.

Another example might be that someone in your life may have told you abusive cruel things about the way you walk or talk or look. They may have made fun of certain physical characteristics or of you as a whole. It could've been a sibling, a parent, a teacher or your peers. After awhile, you started believing they were right.

Now, as an adult, you find that you are obsessive about your looks, or you may diet or exercise to an extreme point. Or you may do self destructive things to your natural beauty because deep inside you feel that you really are ugly. Or maybe you have submitted to several plastic surgery procedures, not because you really wanted them, but because those cruel messages about your nose or your breasts or your thighs kept resounding in your ears. What really happened back in childhood was that you took on a false belief about yourself. You started believing that you were awkward, or ugly, when actually, your energy, all of you, is like nature, perfectly beautiful. And underneath all of your beliefs about being ugly still remains the energy of pure beauty.

So this is your consciousness, your own unique version of the energy that vibrates inside of you, throughout your body and exudes from you. At any given moment of your life, your consciousness is a combination of the pure core energy you started with and all of the beliefs, thoughts and feelings that you took on since then. Your pure core energy is totally an energy of love, abundance, fullness, beauty, health, freedom, power, intelligence, excellence, fulfillment, unlimitedness and harmony with all other life forms. Any area of your life that does not match these adjectives shows that you have added a false belief somewhere to your consciousness.

Earlier, we talked about the fact that each of us has a unique physical expression. Each of us also has a unique consciousness. That's because we all have different thoughts, beliefs, feelings and impressions in our consciousness. And each of those thoughts, beliefs, feelings and impressions carry their own unique kind of energy.

— ACTIONS HAVE ENERGY —

Most of us have been raised to think that our actions have energy. We were taught in school about kinetic, thermal, electric and potential energies. We can see the energy that is transferred from a quarterback's arm to the football as it is thrown down the field. The football doesn't have the energy within itself to throw itself down the field, but the energy passes from the quarterback's arm to the football and we see the effects. It's easy to accept this kind of energy because we learned about it before and we can easily see the results from this kind of energy.

Some of us were also taught about the cause and effect relationship of our actions. The most common phrase associated with this is "what goes around, comes around". We have been taught that if we give out cruelty to others, it will come back to us and if we give out love, the same will happen. All of this is true, although as we will discuss later, sometimes you may think an action is about giving when it is really about taking, or about love when it is really about fear or indifference.

— THOUGHTS HAVE ENERGY —

What may be much harder for you to accept is that your thoughts, beliefs and feelings also have energy associated with them. And as we'll show you later there is also a cause and effect relationship between the circumstances and people in our lives and our thoughts, beliefs and feelings. Let's start by talking about the energy of feelings. Many people have the easiest time accepting this one because they are very sensitive to their own and other people's feelings and they can feel that energy.

— FEELINGS HAVE ENERGY —

Feelings do indeed have energy and the reason some people can feel this energy is because it is not just inside of us. The energy of your feelings radiates in and around you. And you can see and/or feel this, just like you can see and/or feel the results from physical energy. Have you ever had a tender moment of love between you and a lover when the feelings of love between you were so intense that you literally could feel the energy of those feelings in the room? Or maybe you've been in a situation where you walked in on two very angry people. They were too embarrassed to verbalize their anger but you could feel it anyway. Or have you ever been to the funeral of a child? Couldn't you literally feel the grief and sorrow of the family?

Take a few moments now to try an experiment. Kiss the back of your hand. Now, remember what it felt like to be kissed by someone you were madly in love with. Remember the touch upon your lips, the smell in the air and the sounds you heard. It feels very different, doesn't it? The physical actions are basically the same. But the physical action of kissing doesn't feel at all the same when you remove the emotional energy. It's the same when, for whatever reason, you kiss someone for whom you don't have romantic feelings. It's like kissing the back of your hand. It's also a very different feeling when someone kisses you against your will. You see, it's not the action of kissing, but the energy behind the action that colors your experience of it.

Some people may feel like they don't have any feelings. They may have been traumatized and have numbed a lot of their feelings. Other people continually try to hide or mask their feelings. Still others lose sight of what they feel by constantly suppressing their emotions. Regardless, your feelings do have energy. And this energy of your emotions doesn't just go away over time. Western scientists now have shown that emotions are stored in the cells of the body. The thing to remember about your emotions is this: whether you let them be expressed outwardly in the world or you store them up in your body doesn't mean they have any more or less energy surrounding them. Expressing them in some way will just help you to send that energy somewhere else.

So feelings have energy, but where does that energy come from? Let's try another experiment. Think about something that really ticks you off. Think for a moment about your pet peeve in life. It might be a political issue, prejudice, injustice or just the way some people drive their cars. Really center your thoughts for a moment on that pet peeve. Now see how you feel, angry, right? Your blood pressure probably went up, you may have felt your heart beating faster or your body may have tensed up. That is essentially how biofeedback works.

Your thoughts can create not only your feelings, but the physical effects that accompany those feelings. Now, let's try the opposite. Think about a pleasurable experience you have had recently. Remember all the sights, sounds and smells from that experience. Think about how it felt to be touched in that experience, if only by the wind. How do you feel now: relaxed, peaceful, happy? Your thoughts have again created your feelings. What really happens here is that you transform the energy of your thoughts into the energy of your feelings and the physical effects that accompany those feelings.

— IMPRESSIONS —

The energy of your feelings can also be created just by an impression. The feeling of joy may well up in you just by looking at a beautiful ocean sunset or a majestic snow-capped mountain. Everything around us, our experience of the world through our five senses, gives us certain impressions and the energy of these impressions, with or without conscious thoughts, gives us feelings.

Thoughts contain energy just like physical actions and feelings do. A good example of how energy is passed from our thoughts into our reality is psychosomatic illness. We think we are sick and therefore we manifest symptoms to match the energy of those thoughts.

Thoughts take on the energy that is in our conscious mind at the time we think the thought and carry that energy. For example, as you get up to speak publicly, you might think the thought, "I am a confident person". That thought will carry the energy of confidence with it. The intensity of the energy will depend on how much you really believe what it is that you thought. If, deep inside, you believe just the opposite, the positive thought will have very little effect and could in fact carry the energy of self-doubt with it.

Just like feelings, most of us think that our thoughts are something contained only inside of us. We think our thoughts are just contained in our own mind. But the energy of your thoughts radiates in and around your whole body. You might even think of thoughts as being like light or sound waves. Their energy is far reaching like a broadcast signal.

You've probably had the experience of thinking something at the same time as another person and when the other person said it, you exclaimed, "I was just thinking that." Have you ever wondered which one of you really came up with it first? The energy of that thought was both inside and outside of you so anyone was free to pick up the actual thought or maybe just the energy of it. Or have you ever been thinking of someone and later that day they called you? Your thought about them was picked up by them and became a stimulus for them to think about calling you. Or maybe the thought about you originated with them first.

— CORE INTELLIGENCE —

So if your thoughts have energy, then where did that energy come from? Most people believe that thoughts are generated in their mind. Actually, your mind is just the wisdom or intelligence of your core energy. And the energy of your mind is in and around you, not just in one place like in your foot or your brain. Every cell of your body carries the energy of your core intelligence. That's why all of your cells when left in their natural state know exactly what to do to keep you alive and healthy. The energy of your core intelligence and all of the energy you picked up from your experience of life is where the energy of your thoughts comes from. In other words, your core energy and all of the thoughts, beliefs, feelings and impressions that you have allowed to mix in with this energy is where the energy of your thoughts comes from.

Your mind was intended to work as a tool for you, just like a big computer. It seems as though the energy of your thoughts is generated there, but in actuality your mind is just playing back the beliefs and impressions already contained in your consciousness. The energy is not generated in the "computer". It is generated from the energy source that runs the computer. That source is you. Whatever you have put into the computer is what you'll get out. And you are the sole programmer of that computer. Others may try to input, but you have the final say over what is accepted or rejected.

Many people believe that their mind is something out of their control. They may go through life aimlessly allowing everything and everyone else to program their mind. The sad part is that this programming will dictate how they live.

— THE PROGRAMMED MIND —

How does the mind get programmed? One thought or impression is accepted into the mind, and it attracts a like thought or impression. Over time, after many thoughts have been accepted, a belief is formed. Belief is what gives intensity or lack of it to the energy of our thoughts. In fact, beliefs are just thoughts that have been repeated over and over and that's why the energy of a belief is stronger than the energy of an isolated thought. Beliefs have the energy of sometimes hundreds or literally thousands of thoughts compiled within them. The more we hold on to a belief, the more thoughts, impressions and feelings will be attracted into our life to reinforce that belief. The more a belief is reinforced, the stronger the energy behind it and the more effort it will take to change that belief.

That is one reason why so many people end up discouraged with positive thinking. They think that if they just think positively a few times, it'll work magic in their lives. They pile a few positive thoughts in on top of 30 or 40 years of false beliefs. And they try really hard to believe the positive thought. But their underlying beliefs are stronger in intensity, and it will sabotage them every time.

A woman may tell herself that she is beautiful. But, if she has the false belief deep down that she is ugly, it will take a long time for her to change that belief by just telling herself she is beautiful over and over. Using positive thinking alone is like trying to win a foot race with a huge sack of rocks on your back. The faster route to getting what you want is to track down the energy that is already in your consciousness, take a look at it, and when you find false beliefs that are blocking what you want, change that energy. Thinking positive or truthful thoughts can be one tool for changing beliefs, and we'll discuss that later in the book.

What you believe can also be deposited in your consciousness by an action or impression. You don't have to consciously think thoughts about it. Sometimes, it may only take one action or impression for you to form a belief. A child seeing her father slap her mother across the room can cause the child to form beliefs about marriage, men, women and parenting that can last a lifetime. Other times, beliefs are formed from repeated impressions. A child consistently making bad grades in school can easily cause the child to form the belief, over time, that he is stupid.

Tracking down the energy in your consciousness is the hardest part of dealing with your energy and is usually the part we most resist. What makes it more difficult is that we are probably not consciously aware of all of our beliefs. We have grown up accepting the concept of gravity, the rotation of the earth, a myriad of societal pressures and prejudices and we never gave any of it much conscious thought. We may have picked up impressions when our parents divorced, when we received report cards in school, or maybe a major trauma occurred in our childhood. We may have picked up a belief that we are not lovable, or that we are ugly or that God is out to get us. We may not sit and consciously think about these things during the day, but these beliefs nevertheless might be in our consciousness and might be sabotaging us.

Most of us have been conditioned to think that our physical world can have an effect on our mind, body and spirit. We would agree that it is "normal" for a person whose house has just burned down to think and feel thoughts and feelings of sadness and grief. Fewer of us have grown up with the belief that our thoughts, beliefs and feelings can affect conditions in our physical world. But if you can accept that thoughts, beliefs, and feelings all have energy, just like actions, then you will be able to understand more about how their energy works, and you will start to see how that energy creates or manifests physical conditions and circumstances in your life.

Every day, in our normal daily life, during all of our regular daily activities, we are simultaneously broadcasting to the world the energy of our thoughts, feelings and beliefs. We are basically walking-talking broadcast stations. We don't always choose consciously what we broadcast, but we are still always broadcasting. And what are we broadcasting? We are broadcasting the energy of our beliefs, thoughts and feelings, both conscious and unconscious.

— ENERGY ATTRACTS ENERGY —

And this energy that we are all broadcasting, the energy of our consciousness, creates out in our lives, literally everything and everyone that is in our lives. The energy of your consciousness attracts, just like a magnet, a like energy. In other words, whatever kind of energy you put out (or broadcast) will come back to you. So, if your consciousness has lack or limitation beliefs, you will see poverty and money struggles in your life.

Like energy will always attract like energy. It is impossible for the energy of the universe to operate in any other way. Your own unique combination of energy (your consciousness) creates, or attracts, everything and everyone that is in your life in a physical form. Your own unique consciousness attracts in physical form, circumstances and people that are equal to its energy.

As you go about your normal day, you are constantly broadcasting, just like a TV station, the energy of your consciousness to the world. And other people and situations are receiving it, just like TV sets. When the energy you are broadcasting matches a like energy in a person or situation, you will attract him, her or it. And it doesn't have to be all of your energy attracting all of the energy of someone or something else. It can be a tiny portion of your consciousness that attracts a situation or person.

— CONSCIOUSNESS AS BLUEPRINT —

Think of your consciousness as a blueprint for a moment. Blueprints are designs from which to build things. You have a blueprint within yourself, that you designed or allowed others to design, that is constantly creating physical circumstances and attracting people into your life.

One of the hardest things to accept about this is that you are creating your consciousness every moment. You are the one in charge of what goes in and what stays in. And you are the only one who can change what's in your consciousness. The good news is that you have the power within you to change your consciousness and as a result, change your life.

— FRICTION —

Another beautiful part of all of this is that you always attract into your life everything you need to help you uncover all of your false beliefs and get back to who you really are, the wondrous core energy. Our false beliefs attract exactly the right kind of friction we need to cause us to take a look at our consciousness, see where it strayed from the truth and change it back to our true consciousness.

We realize that for some of you the concept of you having created everything in your life may be a hard concept to swallow. After all, you weren't making conscious choices as a baby and even as an adult you haven't always made conscious choices to accept or reject certain beliefs. But the part of your consciousness that you may be unaware of, the unconscious part, the false beliefs, can affect your life without you even knowing it.

Our lives are run by the energy in our belief system and so much of that system is rooted in past influences of which we may not be aware. The challenge here is to be more conscious about the choices we make and to attune ourselves more with our beautiful core energy inside.

If you are willing to take a look at the friction in your life, you can trace it back, see your false beliefs and take steps to change that energy. But if you are unwilling to look at your life, you will continue to attract more and more of the same kind of friction into your life. Eventually the friction will cause you to make changes in your life anyway. The first choice is just less painful than the second choice.

— RELATIONSHIPS —

Relationships provide a particularly useful tool in examining how friction works in our lives. Jimmie remembers some of his earlier relationships being painful: "My tendency was to blame my partners for the pain. What I realized in later years is that I was a big part of my own pain. I had only learned how to take and not give. And I was running from the fear of failure. It was all disguised in the socially acceptable guise of being the perfect male provider, the overworked business executive. The friction and pain increased in both my personal and business lives with the pain of divorce and bankruptcy being the end product. How much easier it would have all been if I had just been aware of what my false beliefs on the inside were creating for me on the outside. I could have changed that energy and saved myself a lot of pain."

It would be nice if we could have a blueprint of our consciousness that we could lay out on the kitchen table. We would be able to see all the false beliefs we had actively written in or allowed to be drawn in on our blueprint. It would make it so easy to trace an unpleasant event in the present back to a false belief deposited in the past. It isn't always that easy. The blueprint of our consciousness isn't something we can examine on an empty table. Like the iceberg, much of it is hidden from us and, to make matters worse, we sometimes resist learning about the hidden part. But each day, if you become more aware of yourself, of what's in your consciousness, you will find yourself closer and closer to achieving your dreams.

RESPONSIBILITY

*We've learned about the fact that we are made of energy
and that our energy attracts, like a magnet, circumstances
and people of like energy.*

*Some of you may have already done extensive work on yourselves
to release the false beliefs that were deposited on your blueprint.
Others of you have never taken any steps at all to examine
your consciousness. In any case, just take a minute to think
about all of the beliefs, all of the philosophies,
all of the thoughts of all of the people that were around you as a child.
Think about the impressions that other people's actions made on you.
Think about how easy it was for you to absorb all of this
into your consciousness.*

— MESSAGES —

What messages did you get from your parents, from your siblings, from your relatives? What messages did you get from school, from your teachers, from your counselors, from your peers? What about dating, or not having any dates? What kinds of messages were passed on to you about your sexuality? What about the kinds of messages our society gave you about your looks or the neighborhood you lived in? What kinds of messages did you get from your church, from your spiritual leaders? What about TV? What kinds of messages did you get from the media? What kinds of messages did you hear from the music you listened to?

This is not an attempt to list all the messages that you may have received in childhood that could have had an effect on you or that could be affecting your life now. We have just listed some examples to get you thinking about the myriad of messages and countless circumstances that may have been a stimulus for you to form a false belief about yourself.

Remember, your natural state, your core energy, is about abundance, fullness, beauty, health, intelligence, freedom, power, excellence, fulfillment, unlimitedness and harmony. Think for a minute. Were you around messages or circumstances that made you feel wealthy and abundant, loved, beautiful, smart, free, unlimited, in harmony with others?

If you weren't, and most of us weren't, then you need to start thinking about what kinds of messages you were around as a child because chances are they became part of your blueprint, part of your consciousness. Also think about what kinds of messages you expose yourself to now. What kinds of people do you hang out with? What kinds of music do you listen to? What kind of TV programs do you watch? What kinds of books or magazines do you read?

The main point you need to realize, then, is that we do create our own lives. How? We attract a like energy in the form of people and/or circumstances that in some way matches our consciousness, or blueprint.

You may say, "I didn't put those messages in my consciousness. How did they get there?" That's a good question and one that we don't know all the answers to. We do know that children generally accept whatever is told to them, especially if it is told to them over and over. And most of us were taught as children to accept society's values without question, or the church's values, or our parents' values.

Whatever the case, we may not have actively or consciously added a belief to our consciousness. We probably didn't say to ourselves, "I'm going to live my life by this belief from now on". We may have just allowed it to be deposited in our consciousness by someone else. We may have allowed the actions of others to give us a false impression. That's why it's important to look at the messages you got from childhood, because that's generally where our false beliefs got started.

No matter how the false beliefs got started, you are still responsible for your own consciousness. You are still the one that creates your own life. Jimmie remembers being very sad when he finally realized this. It was easier to place the responsibility on God, or his past or someone else. It was easier to be a victim.

— VICTIMISM —

Before we go any farther, we'd like to define victim as placing the responsibility for an event, incident or circumstance on something outside of yourself. You can place it on someone or something else, but being a victim means that you deny having any part in the manifestation of the people and/or circumstances in your life. Listen to the way we talk in our society. "It was my husband's fault." "The policeman wouldn't listen." "My boss was not understanding." "The economy was bad." "The government wouldn't do anything about it." "The Japanese won't make fair trade agreements."

Many people these days are talking about taking responsibility for their own lives. But we believe you are responsible for your life, whether you accept that responsibility or not. Webster's defines responsibility as "accountable, as being the cause of". That is exactly what we are talking about.

It is your energy, your consciousness, that causes or attracts all of the people and circumstances in your life. You have a few choices. You can go along with your life without ever accepting responsibility and you will continue attracting your own particular brand of friction, your own pattern of troubles. This can be very painful because you end up repeating the same patterns of poverty, hatred, limitedness, disharmony, stress or failure. What's worse is that the repetition of these patterns leaves you feeling powerless. You feel like something outside of yourself is the cause and you are powerless to stop it.

The other choice is to take a look at your life and take responsibility for it by looking inside to see what part your energy, your consciousness, is playing. Then you can make changes. You can take a look at the energy in your life, transform that energy and therefore change your life. The first choice is about victimism and the second choice is about empowerment. You can't be a victim and be empowered at the same time.

Does this mean that being a victim is wrong or bad? Absolutely not! We don't ever want to give you that impression. There are seasons for everything. In the 1960's, the Byrds had a song with the verse, "To everything there is a season, turn, turn, turn," which was based on a Bible verse from Ecclesiastes. We all need periods of time for both sides of the coin. We need the balance of victimism and responsibility in our lives. To live constantly engrossed in either would be unbalanced and painful. We also need the balance of our responsibility versus other's responsibility. Responsibility never lies completely on one side or the other.

If you are the kind of person who has never taken a look at the other side of the coin, your responsibility for creating your own life, then it might be time for a season of that. If you are the kind of person who has always taken complete responsibility for everything and everybody, it might be time for you to focus on other people's responsibility. The point is to live in a mode where you make conscious choices about the way you are living.

Let's talk about why someone would want or need to spend a season being a victim. Sometimes, people need to get into a victim state in order to flush out stuck emotions. Those emotions carry with them a certain kind of energy which might otherwise sabotage that person's life. If they don't release those emotions, they might turn that energy against themselves or might never be able to move on in their lives, just repeating a cycle of destructive patterns. Many people who aren't really in touch with their emotions are suffering from stuck emotions they are afraid to look at and they need a season of victimism to get them out. Others have turned the emotions into self-destructive patterns, but don't know how to quit the cycle.

A good example of this is abuse victims. First of all, many abuse victims blame themselves for what happened to them. They focus all the responsibility for the abuse on themselves. They carry this energy around, subconsciously punishing themselves for what happened. A season of being a victim helps them to focus on someone or something outside of themselves and helps them to quit blaming themselves. As they place responsibility on their abuser, they can get angry, feel the pain and feel the helplessness. They can literally see that this energy is not their own energy. It is the energy of the abuser that they took on and they can psychically send that energy back where it came from and find their own pure energy again.

Barbara remembers abuse from her childhood: "I was constantly abused by one of my brothers, especially physically and verbally. He told me so many ugly things about myself that I truly believed I was the ugliest urchin to ever crawl upon this earth. I felt utterly power-less and terrified when I was around him.

"As an adult, I finally got into therapy, and I went through a real season of being a victim. I got angry, even rageful toward my brother. I blamed him for all the problems I had experienced with the men in my life. I even went so far as to confront him with what he had done to me. The most important thing I did in therapy was to finally understand that it was his energy, not my own pure energy, that I had taken on in my consciousness. The things he had taught me about myself were not true. All of those impressions he had made on me about me being powerless and ugly were really projections of his own energy and the way he felt about himself. All of the energy of my false beliefs about myself came from him, not me. Once I realized all of this, I spent many years in meditation, consciously separating myself from this energy and sending it back to him."

Sometimes after a traumatic event, people need a season of vic-timism because responsibility is just too hard to digest at that time. Jimmie remembers an event from his life in that way: "I got fired from a job and I blamed literally almost everyone in the company for my firing. It took me several weeks before I saw that I did have a part in attracting and creating the situation. I'm glad I went through that season of victimism because immediately after the firing, my self-esteem took a hit. Not taking responsibility for it right away gave me a chance to start healing my self-esteem. After my self-esteem was stronger, I was able to take a look at the part I played in it."

Being a victim elicits nurturing from others. Sometimes that is exactly what we need at the time. If you feel that you need this, don't try to rush through this period in your life. Allow others to validate your feelings and nurture you. You can always move on to what part you played in the situation at a later date.

Jimmie remembers a time in his life where he needed to be a victim and just receive some nurturing: "I had moved to New York after ending a 15 year career in real estate. I watched trusted friends and colleagues abandon me as my company fell apart. I felt confused and I had a hard time taking a look at my responsibility in the matter. I filled my life with activities in New York, so many activities that I didn't have time to think or feel.

"Then I met Barbara and, over time, her love allowed me to open up to my own feelings. For the first time I was able to feel the deeply painful hurt that accompanies betrayal. I reached a point where I had a decision to make. I could continue in my frenzied career and social activities, or I could move back to Louisiana where Barbara was and be nurtured by her love. I remember thinking, 'my soul needs to be watered by Barbara's love so that I can grow'. I moved to Louisiana to be with Barbara, and there I found an environment where I felt comfortable being myself and feeling all of my feelings. In this environment, I was able to feel all of the hurt and the pain as Barbara's loving nurturance and acceptance of me helped me back into life. What I needed at that point in my life was to be a victim, feel my feelings and have all of that lovingly validated."

In our society, victimism has become the catalyst for change. We need people in our society who are willing to point fingers and scream about injustice before our society or our government is willing to make changes. You can look at some of the past changes and see that without victimism we would still be in the dark ages about chauvinism and racial and sexual prejudice.

So you can see that there are two ways to focus on every situation. You can focus on everyone else's responsibility or you can focus on your own. If you are not ready to focus on your own, that's O.K. No one can tell you how long your season for focusing on other's responsibility should be. No one can tell you how bad a problem should be before you speak out and point fingers to shake things up and create change. If you've recently been through a terrible trauma it may take years for you to heal. Just stay with the path that feels right for you.

— FEELING EMPOWERED —

Now, having said that, let us give you some good reasons for getting through your victimism and getting on with your own responsibility. However long you stay in the role of the victim is how long you will not feel empowered in your life. If you think the problem is outside of you, then you have to wait for someone or something outside of yourself to fix the problem. You may wait a long time, and all the time you are waiting, you will not feel empowered. For your life to feel empowered, you must feel as though you have some control over your own destiny. The wondrous energy source that is at the core of everyone is very powerful. In other words, we all have the power to change our own lives. That is, we all have the power unless we choose to give that power up to someone or something else, which is what you have to do to be a victim.

If you hang on to your victim role, you will feel helpless to keep the same kind of trauma from happening again. On the other hand, if you uncover your part in the situation, you have the opportunity to change that energy and prevent yourself from attracting the same types of situations or people.

Barbara remembers a person she attracted in her life this way: "I was very much in love with a man who was cheating on me. At first, I complained to all of my friends about him and went through a total season of being a victim. I finally ended the relationship, even though it was incredibly painful for me to do so. Years later, I realized that his cheating on me was not one sided. I had a part in creating the situation. I realized that I had always subjugated my needs to his. I had also allowed him to treat me with disrespect verbally. This kind of energy said to him, 'it's okay for you to treat me any way you want and put your needs ahead of mine.' That is exactly what I attracted. I attracted a situation where he was putting his needs ahead of mine. The good part is that after I saw my part in this painful affair, I worked on the energy in my consciousness, and I started attracting men who gave to me and treated me with respect."

— CONFLICT —

Conflict is never about one person or one side. Conflict is always about both people and both sides. Your part in the conflict may be small, but nevertheless, you will gain back your feeling of power if you can figure out what your part in the conflict is. Even if your only contribution to the conflict is allowing or attracting it, you will feel much more empowered if you acknowledge your part because you can then change your consciousness and never again attract or allow the same kinds of people or circumstances into your life.

If you constantly blame other people or your circumstances and never get into your own responsibility, you will stay in a vicious cycle of helplessness. The more helpless you feel, the more you blame others. The more you blame others, the more helpless you feel. Why? You can't change other people or their consciousness and oftentimes you can't change your immediate situation either. You can only change yourself and the false beliefs you have about yourself. Even if you manage to consciously avoid or eliminate certain types of people or situations from your life, you will find that essentially the same types of people and situations will keep popping up in your life until you change your own consciousness.

— ENERGY OF VICTIMISM —

Another reason to move beyond victimism is because victimism breeds fear. When you place yourself in the role of the victim, you will always be afraid that the same kind of person or circumstance can happen to you again. You will end up living in fear instead of peace. If you take responsibility for your life, you will see that the person or circumstance in your life was attracted there by your own consciousness. Therefore, you can change your consciousness and never again attract this kind of person or situation into your life. By taking responsibility for everything in your life, you are choosing to live in peace instead of fear.

Victimism can even be dangerous to our society and can seal your fate towards unpleasant circumstances. When someone sees him or herself as the victim, they can literally rationalize any of their own behavior as "someone else's fault." Whatever they might do to other people, for that they carry around a built in excuse. As they focus on their victimism, it magnifies their feelings of helplessness which causes them to react with all kinds of irrational and destructive behaviors.

An extreme example of this would be the cases we have seen on the news where someone has walked into a building and shot several other people. When asked about the incident, the shooter always talks in terms of what someone else did to them. It was because of the mean boss that fired them or the spouse that left them. People can be harmed and the shooter's fate in prison can be sealed all because of their victimism. All cases don't have to be this extreme. Many marriages break up because one party or the other feels victimized and, therefore, feels vindicated in saying or doing something so unforgivable that the marriage has to end.

We have noticed that our entire society appears to have been stuck in victimism for quite some time. Our society seems to actually condone and support victimism. Our society as a whole acts and thinks in terms of being a victim and therefore, it becomes all too easy for us to live our own individual lives that way. But as each person starts taking responsibility for creating his or her own life, then we as a society will change also and start taking responsibility for what happens to us as a society.

— VICTIMISM SEPARATES —

One of the main reasons you may want to get past your victimism is because it separates you rather than brings you into harmony with others. In order to be a victim, you must thrust responsibility, judgment, and blame outward from yourself on to others. Judgment will always separate. You will always turn away from anything or anyone that judges you.

Your natural state is to be in harmony with other living beings. If you are judging others, you will be causing separation, and you will be out of your natural state. Anytime you are out of your natural state you will be at the very least uncomfortable and at the very worst, in pain. Remember, too, that blame has to do with an energy of resisting your own responsibility, and therefore, it will attract resistance from the one being blamed. Nothing is ever resolved with this kind of energy, and nothing can be accomplished between conflicted parties. It is only in the coming together of all people, who are willing to take some responsibility in the issues, that we can finally find real answers and all of us can live in our natural state of harmony.

— ENERGY OF RESPONSIBILITY —

We've taken a look at the energy of victimism. Now let's take a look at the energy of responsibility. The energy of responsibility says, "I want more of this in my life." Let's take an example of two teenagers, both of whom have a new car. One teenager takes great care of his car. He washes it, waxes it and vacuums it regularly. He doesn't let his drunk friends drive it. He parks it in safe places. He gets regular maintenance done on it. His thoughts are of thankfulness and appreciation for his car. This teenager has thoughts and actions of responsibility. His energy says, "I want more of this in my life". This kind of energy will eventually attract circumstances where he will keep this car or get an even better one.

Let us look at the other teenager. He never washes, waxes or vacuums his car. In fact, his car looks like the garbage from a fast food restaurant was dumped inside. He doesn't care who drives it. He doesn't care where he parks it. He takes having a car for granted and never performs any maintenance on the car. Yet, this same teen would be very shocked and feel victimized if his car broke down, was stolen or was wrecked. He would probably blame someone or something else. It was the fault of the manufacturer, his friend or some thief. But his actions and his thoughts were about irresponsibility towards the car. His energy said, "I want less of this in my life." The circumstances will match the energy coming from the person and, therefore, this teen may end up with a broken or wrecked car or no car at all. No matter how much he says he wants a new car in his life, it will be hard for him to attract another one until he understands this lesson and changes his inner messages of irresponsibility. Unless he is rescued out of these circumstances by other people, what he will attract is less and less of a nice car until it exactly reaches his level of irresponsibility.

Does this mean that the first teen will never have his car break down, be wrecked or stolen? No, it just means that he has put out an energy that says "I want a nice car." It's as if he has built a nest, a safe haven, a nurturing receptacle for his desires to fly home to. He has done everything he can do to make the vibration of a nice car feel welcome in his life.

— RESPONSE-ABILITY —

Responsibility is really our "ability to respond." It is our way of putting energy out into the universe that shows what we want more or less of in our lives. And the energy in the universe will respond back with circumstances/people/things that match the essence of the energy you put out. This doesn't mean that you always get whatever you want if you are just responsible about it. You may have false beliefs that block you from getting it, your desire may be fulfilled at a later time, or your desire may be fulfilled in a different way than you expected.

We have a very good example of this from our own lives. Over two years time we spent over $10,000 in doctor bills, shots, and pills in order for us to have children. Barbara finally got pregnant with triplets. She stopped drinking all alcoholic drinks even during the time she was trying to get pregnant as well as during the pregnancy. She only ate healthy foods. She watched every morsel of food she put in her mouth to make sure there wasn't something more nutritious she could be eating. She stayed on bed rest for months, lying on her side and even eating meals on her side.

Barbara remembers, "Jimmie went to every doctor's appointment with me. He played a part in every decision. He even slept on the floor of my hospital room once I was admitted to the hospital. Once the triplets were born, Jimmie spent every waking hour either by my side or with the babies."

In the end, all three of the babies died from prematurity. So, even though everything we did in the situation was a responsible move, we still don't have the children we wanted. It's been six months since the last baby died, and we still don't have all of the answers. It

could be that we have some false beliefs that we have yet to uncover
that are blocking us from getting the children we want. It could be
that we will have children at another time in our lives. It could be
that our desire to have children will be fulfilled by another path.

We do know this. The energy of responsibility is about peace.
Look at our example above. If we hadn't done everything we possibly could to insure the health of our children, and let them know
how much we loved and wanted them, just imagine what guilt and
shame would be mixed in with our grief.

What about the example of the teenager with the car? The first
teen probably spent very few moments of his life in stress and worry
over his car, because he knew that he had been responsible with it.
Haven't you ever been to a party and had to park your car in a not-
so-safe place? During the entire party, a part of your mind was on
your car and deep in worry. Whether he would admit it or not, the
second teenager had a part of him constantly worried.

Or maybe you spent just one night in passionate unprotected
sex. If you did, you can't deny that you've had many moments of fear,
stress and worry because of that one night. Irresponsibility invites
fear, stress, and guilt. Responsibility invites peace.

Responsibility doesn't just involve individuals. We as a society
are also responsible. We recently vacationed in Destin, Florida over
the July 4th holiday. Arguably, Destin Beach is one of the most beautiful beaches in America. It has about 150 feet of beautiful white

bleached sands that lead into crystal clear, emerald green, warm gulf waters. We were saddened and shocked when we walked on the beach early the morning of July 5th. We saw the remains of roman candles, firecrackers and beer cans floating in that beautiful ocean, not to mention the trashed beach. That kind of energy of irresponsibility towards our earth and its beauty will eventually get us less of a beautiful earth to look at and enjoy.

Many of us have thought of responsibility as an ugly word, but responsibility is a very beautiful thing. Responsibility broken down to its essence is your ability to respond to the world. By the energy of your thoughts and actions, which spring from your inner beliefs, you show your world whether you want more or less of a possession, person or situation in your life. The things, people or situations that you don't take care of, take for granted, take unnecessary risks with or are unappreciative of will degenerate or disappear from your life.

When Jimmie got fired, one of the things that he learned about himself and the part he played in getting fired, was that he had been taking his job for granted. He was unappreciative of his job and he had been taking unnecessary risks with his job. This irresponsible energy he put out was a factor in his firing. He put out energy of "I don't want this in my life" and that's what he got.

Sometimes we aren't ready for a person, possession or situation in our lives and although our desire may attract it into our lives, our energy of irresponsibility pushes it away. As a sales manager, Barbara has known many sales representatives who have put out an energy of irresponsibility toward their job and were fired. She has known several of them who were hired at approximately the same salary and responsibility level several years later. What probably happened is that they weren't ready for that level of responsibility the first time around, but they obviously worked on that and later played it out differently the second time around.

Even though at first you may meet with some resistance to the idea of taking responsibility for everything and everyone in your life, let us tell you the good news. The good news is that if you take responsibility for creating or attracting literally everything in your life, then you can also un-create or quit attracting the parts that you don't like. Taking responsibility for your life brings more power and peace to your life. It also helps to remove the fear.

— THE FIRST STEP —

The first step in creating what you want in your life is to realize that you have already created or attracted everything that is in your life now. So if you have a husband who pays you no attention, he is someone your consciousness attracted. And the dead end job that you hate is what your consciousness created. And the constant battle you have with the bills is about your belief in lack.

Every painful experience in life can be traced back to an untrue belief about yourself. Somewhere inside of you are beliefs, thoughts or impressions or a combination of the three, that are not about love, abundance, fullness, beauty, health, freedom, power, excellence, fulfillment, unlimitedness and harmony. And those untrue beliefs, thoughts or impressions are attracting an experience of like energy.

Jimmie can trace a lot of the pain in his life back to age six to an experience that changed the way he saw the world for many years to come: "I was sleeping in my bedroom that I shared with my younger brother, then about four, when I began to be pulled from my peaceful sleep by what sounded like so much turmoil that it seemed like the whole world was coming to an end. I remember lying there feeling absolutely terrified when I suddenly realized that it was my parents screaming at each other at the top of their lungs. At that moment, I sank down in my bed with a feeling of depression, of sadness, that would stay with me for years to come. I am not telling you about this so that we can examine what my mom and dad were doing. I want to talk about my part of the experience and the energy involved.

"Up until that point in my life, as far as I can tell, my view of the world was pretty much one of this being a safe place to be. Years later, with lots of therapy and introspection, I realized that I formed the belief that night that something must be wrong with me.

"Who knows how a six year old child's mind cognizes things, but it went something like this. If my parents were fighting like this, it must be my fault. I must not have been good enough. There must be something wrong with me. And if my parents scared me so much that night, to my very core, then they must not love me. And certainly they wouldn't ever be there to protect me because they weren't protecting me now. And if they weren't going to love and protect me, then I would have to do it all by myself. To make matters worse, I later realized that I somehow got my concept of God all wrapped up in that night. It registered in my consciousness that if my parents didn't love me, then neither did God. And if my parents wouldn't protect me, then neither would God.

"So without consciously knowing it, back at age six, I formed beliefs about myself, my parents and God. I believed from that point on that neither God nor my parents loved me. I felt something was wrong with me, and that the world was a bad, scary place. I believed I had to be perfect to hopefully convince God and my parents to love me. I was convinced that I had to watch every detail of my life because I was the only one protecting myself.

"As you can imagine, I spent the rest of my life trying to control literally everything and everyone in an attempt to be perfect and to keep every detail under my control. This ended up with me becoming obsessive about everything. My life as an adult was full of worry, fear and obsessions. It got so bad that at one point I went into a residential treatment center for help.

"It would have been easy for me to trace all of this back and blame my adult troubles on my parents. I have taken a season to do just that so that I could get rid of all of the anger, the fear and the helplessness. But then I started to take responsibility for my life. I traced all of the things in my life that I didn't like back to a false belief that I allowed to be deposited in my consciousness. I saw where I had formed beliefs, most of them unconscious, that had attracted people and circumstances into my life. I began to change those beliefs and to take actions which matched my new beliefs. The fear, worry and obsessions that marked most of my adult life began to vanish."

Some questions that often come up for people when they are learning about taking responsibility for their lives are, "What about the person or situation that hurt or abused me? Shouldn't they take responsibility for what they did?" Or, "Why should I take responsibility for my part in this, when the person who abused me doesn't even think they did anything wrong?"

We are not saying that any of the hurtful behavior that one human inflicts on another is innocent, excusable or right. They acted from their own set of false beliefs. And you can't change those false beliefs for them or change their consciousness in any way. If you do try to do that you are hanging on to the energy that hurt you in the first place.

In fact, you don't have to worry whether they will change or not. We assure you, their energy will attract circumstances and people that are specifically designed to eliminate their false beliefs and get them back to their natural state of love. To admit your own responsibility in a matter does not diminish anyone else's responsibility in the same matter.

Your part may have just been one of unconsciously allowing or attracting a person or situation. Your part may have just been having such a low level of self love that you attracted a like energy in the form of abuse. What we're saying here is that only by acknowledging your own responsibility in having a person or circumstance in your life, will you ever live with empowerment and peace. You don't do it for them. You do it for yourself.

— ENERGY OF REVENGE —

This seems like a good time to talk about the energy of revenge. Many people think that they must "get back" at a person who has hurt or wronged them. Again, sometimes this can be therapeutic by allowing a person to get rid of some of their anger, pain and helplessness. But after the anger is gone, a very powerful way of dealing with someone who has hurt you is to realize your part in the situation, change your own consciousness and believe in the principles of the energy at work.

Remember, whatever kind of energy another person has put out will come back to them. If someone cheats you, it will come back to them. If someone abuses you, that will also come back to them. You don't have to control it. That is simply one of the laws of energy.

Barbara had a good example of this in her life: "I bought a house with a man I'll call Marty. This was my dream house. I couldn't think of anything else I'd ever want in a house. When Marty and I split up,

I couldn't afford to pay the house notes by myself, so I moved out. Marty and I agreed on a dollar amount to be paid to me for my share of the house equity. I went ahead and signed the sales documents, even though Marty had not paid me the money. Years went by and Marty never paid me. Several times I asked him for the money, but there was always an excuse. My friends and family wanted me to do something to get back at Marty. I refused even though the thought was tempting. I knew that Marty's energy would come back to him and so would mine. I also began to take responsibility for my part in the situation. I realized that I chose to sign the sales papers without being paid, thereby taking care of Marty's needs and not my own. I decided to work on my own consciousness instead of exacting revenge.

"Three years later, I ran into Marty in an elevator, and he asked if I had any interest in getting the house back. At this point in my life, I was married to Jimmie and together we could afford the notes. We worked out a deal to buy back the house at below market value because real estate had fallen over those three years and I was able to get the money that was owed to me put into the deal. My trusting of the principles of energy rather than trying to get revenge resulted in my getting back my dream house."

This is not to say that you should not stand up for yourself when you are in the midst of mistreatment or abuse. It is a very self-loving act to always take care of yourself. And self-love is one of the highest forms of energy that exists. As Barbara puts it: "The absolute best thing that could have been done was for me to stand up for myself in the beginning. Instead, I took care of Marty and signed the sales papers even though he did not have the money to pay me. However, I recognized this as my own lack of self love and I refused to give in to the energy of revenge."

Revenge is a very different kind of energy than standing up for yourself in the moment. Revenge is a "getting back" or "hurtful" kind of energy. Not only will it keep you wrapped up in hurtful energy instead of going on with your life, but it will also bring hurtful energy back into your life.

This is also not to say that criminals should be set free or that we should not prosecute them. The kind of energy that criminals put out will come back to them. However, the laws of energy may work slowly or quickly. Therefore, it is a self- loving act of our society to have consequences for anyone who disobeys our laws. It is also a loving act for someone who was traumatized by another human to testify against them and keep them from hurting other human beings. The criminal justice system is just a tool that quickly returns the energy a criminal puts out, back to them.

— "ACCIDENTS" —

Another question that usually comes up for people when they are learning about taking responsibility for their lives is, "Do you mean it was not an accident when that plane crashed"? Of course, it was an accident, just like when you fall and break your arm. It's an accident, as such, but it's an accident that was attracted by a person's or several people's energy. Jimmie had an accident recently where he fell off his bicycle. He wanted to ride the bike, but our 100 pound Weimerainer wanted to go along.

Jimmie remembers it like this: "I knew Max had the power to pull me off the bike, but I chose to take him along anyway. We only got about 10 feet down the road before my face was meeting the pavement. I later realized that I placed Max's desires ahead of my own safety. In other words, I was putting out an energy of non-self-love. What I got back was an equal energy of non-self-love in the form of a scar on my chin."

Everything in your life can be traced back to the ever progressing march of your wondrous core energy that is throwing off all the false beliefs you hold about yourself. As you move though life, you can choose to get rid of more and more of those false beliefs by taking responsibility for having them in your consciousness in the first place. You can choose to admit your part in attracting or creating everything and everyone in your life. Of course, you can also choose to have seasons of being a victim as well. Just make sure that you eventually move on to taking responsibility for your life so that you can get on with creating everything you consciously want in your life.

DESIRE

It was on a quiet beach in Hawaii several years ago
when we both began to work with desires as a couple.
Jimmie had spent a lifetime suppressing his desires
in favor of what he thought was the "right" thing to do.
Barbara, on the other hand, had been alive with desire all of her life,
yet was still thwarted by hidden blocks inside her
that were keeping her from having what she wanted.
Over the next several years, we both learned many lessons
about how to get what we really wanted.

— THE UNIVERSE —

One of the first things we had to address was our concept of God, Goddess, a higher power, wondrous energy source of the universe, or whatever label you choose to use. For the purposes of this book we will simply call this magnificent energy source, the Universe. Please note the capital letter used to distinguish it from the scientific use of the word. We had to address questions like why does the Universe allow all the suffering in the world? Does the Universe create it or do we also create it? Why do some people seem to get what they want and other people don't? Why are so many people unhappy with their lives? Where do desires come from in the first place? Are some desires wrong or bad?

— THE UNIVERSITY OF LIFE —

To answer some of these questions, we must first deal with the entire concept of life, or in other words, "Why am I here?" If you can, for a moment, let yourself imagine that being human, being on this planet, is like being in a giant university. All you are here for is to learn. And we are all enrolled in the same curriculum, yet we may be taking different courses at different times. There are no grades and no failure. So there's no need to cheat or try to get ahead of anyone else. Everyone graduates because the goal is learning. And you will learn, whether you choose to learn on a conscious level or not.

Your understanding is not necessary to bring about change in your life. Learning from a conscious mode just makes the courses easier for you. And your learning is all that you take with you when you leave this planet. That's the way the school's designed. We are all here to learn the same thing. We are here to learn about who we really are inside.

Our curriculum is about learning that we are made of the energy of love, abundance, fullness, beauty, health, freedom, power, excellence, fulfillment, unlimitedness, intelligence and harmony. And the wondrous energy source that is inside of all of us is in charge of your learning. The wondrous energy source inside of you is constantly moving you towards your natural state in all the areas of your life. The best part is that there are no consequences for not learning a lesson. If you refuse to learn a particular lesson, you will just attract a different set of circumstances or people that will help to teach you the same lesson in a different way.

Sometimes if we are stuck in a particular course or we consistently resist the learning, we will attract some crisis or accident into our lives to get us moving again. We have all heard accounts of people who nearly died in a car or plane crash and it literally changed their lives. After the accident, they took inventory of their life and made some drastic changes in the way they were living. We have also heard of people who attracted a disease that caused them to dramatically alter their lifestyle and their mindset. Sometimes we attract these types of situations in order to get us back on track with our curriculum of learning. Also, sometimes we attract a painful situation because we weren't listening when the less painful lessons were presented. And sometimes we attract a painful situation to make us appreciate what we have. But even the learning that seems painful is all accomplished with our highest good in mind.

Imagine what it must be like for a small child who requires surgery for some reason. The child has no idea of what is going on much less the reason for the surgery. In the end, the surgery is successful and although there was pain and discomfort the child is back happily involved in life. This is very similar to our experiences as an adult when we sometimes don't know exactly why something emotionally or physically painful is happening. Whether we realize it or not, there will always be growth and changes even though they are sometimes so subtle that we don't even realize we've changed. We can always trust that our core energy is ever leading us toward learning about ourselves for our own good in the unique way that only works for us.

— DESIRE —

Since the learning starts with desire, let's first define desire. Webster's defines it as "a wish or a longing for". We all may wish for a hundred things a day so that's not what we're talking about. In our context, we would like to make the distinction between desires and whims. We would like you to think of desire as a longing for that never seems to go away. A whim would be more like "I wish I could get a closer parking place" or "I'd like a new dress" or "I'd like to win my tennis match this morning". For most of us, our desires would have more depth and they would be like a gnawing inside of us that recurs over a period of time. Our desires would be something that seems to come from our very core.

Our desires when distilled to their essence are always about the energy of one of our natural attributes. So, your wanting a better job might be about your natural state of fulfillment. And your wanting to own your own beautiful house might be about wanting to get back to your natural state of abundance. And your wanting a solid love relationship in your life could be about your desire to express your natural state of love.

Our desires are always trying to lead us back to our pure core energy. If we will just follow our natural desires, they will motivate us to change our lives back to our natural states of abundance, excellence, power, love and all of our other natural attributes. Oftentimes, we've gotten this energy so covered up in false beliefs and attitudes that we must first uncover it and get rid of the false beliefs before we can have what we truly desire. That's where the school comes in. No matter how tough the courses ahead of you look, rest assured that the Universe is always moving towards giving you what you want and fulfilling your desires.

Let's take an example here of a single guy we know who really wants love in his life. He is ready, he thinks, to share his life with someone. He can't understand why he keeps meeting the same kind of women that take advantage of him and then drop him like a hot potato. He wants love in his life and the Universe wants him to have love in his life, too. You see, the Universe, which is expressing as him, is always moving Itself toward the purest expression of Itself. What he doesn't see is that these women that keep appearing in his life are women that he has attracted by his own consciousness.

In other words, the self-love he has for himself exactly matches the kind of women or love he is attracting into his life. He also doesn't see that if he worked on his own energy of self-love, got rid of whatever false beliefs he has about himself and replaced those with the truth about his nature, he would start attracting more women who would equal that same kind of energy. In other words, by loving himself more, he would attract women who would also show him more love.

In our example above, all the man may see is the pain that these women have brought into his life. Therein lies the first step. In order to start creating what you really want in life, you must stop labeling experiences or other people as good or bad. And you must stop blaming others for all of your pain.

Remember that the goal here is learning, and you can learn from a pleasant or a painful experience. If you label an experience or a person as bad, you will tend to blame the situation or the person for your pain. Your pain really comes from being less than or other than your true nature of love, abundance, fullness, beauty, health, freedom, power, excellence, fulfillment, unlimitedness, intelligence and harmony.

If the man in our example had energy of total self-love, he would not have attracted the women who took advantage of him in the first place. If he places all the blame on them for the problem, he won't learn about his own energy and his consciousness won't change. Therefore his consciousness will continue attracting the same kind of friction or pain in his life. It may come in a different form, but it will still be about his lack of self-love.

Actually, this university of life is a very loving system. Nothing is intended to be a struggle for us or to hurt us. All of our lessons are intended to be taught without pain. We may make them painful because we refuse to listen to what is being taught. Or we may resist what we know to be true. Or there may be absolutely no other way for this lesson to be taught. A parent sometimes has to watch a young child go through something painful in order for the child to learn. And very lovingly the parent makes the child face the learning because they know the child will be better off after they have learned that particular lesson. In the same way, The Universe very lovingly brings friction into our lives so that we can learn the very beautiful lesson of who we really are inside. And what beautiful lessons they are. All of our lessons teach us about our magnificent, beautiful true nature.

— RESISTANCE CREATES PAIN —

Here is another principle of energy. When you resist something, you increase the pain. Take, for example, when a physician is giving you a shot. If you tense up your muscles and resist the shot, it will probably hurt more than if you just relaxed. It's the same with the learning that takes place in our lives. Whenever we resist the learning, the people and circumstances we will attract will be more painful than before. The Universe will have to use pain to get our attention. In other words, the learning gets harder until we learn that particular lesson. The converse is also true, when we don't resist the learning, the people and circumstances we will attract will be less painful. When we welcome the learning, our lessons won't have to be as painful. We can usually learn what we need to know through pleasant experiences.

When we resist people or circumstances that we have attracted into our lives, generally the resistance or the fear is much worse than actually facing what is before us. When Barbara was in the hospital before and after the triplets were born, every day she was faced with another painful test that the doctors wanted to perform. What she found out was that her fear of the painfulness of each of the events was much worse than actually going through them. She finally reached a point where she quit resisting whatever the doctors wanted, and she found that nothing was quite as painful as the dread or fear of something painful.

Barbara also remembers a time in her life where she carried around a consciousness lacking in self-love and full of low self-esteem. She now sees how that kind of energy attracted very abusive men into her life, and she sees how her resistance to the learning made the lessons harder and more painful.

"I went around for years complaining that I couldn't find any nice men. I even went to counseling because I had such a strong desire to have a stable, loving relationship with a man. Even though the counselor encouraged me to look at myself, I was convinced that I was just meeting the wrong kind of men or that God just wasn't answering my prayers. In other words, I placed all the blame for all the failed relationships on the men or on a God that just didn't like me enough to give me what I wanted.

"I started out attracting irresponsible and dishonest men. Then, when I didn't get the lesson that I needed to work on my own level of self-love, the lessons got harder. I ended up attracting several instances of getting raped on dates. And I hit bottom when I married a man who physically and verbally abused me.

"Finally, after an abusive incident with my now ex-husband, something inside of me snapped. I realized that I was a lovely person inside and deserved better than this. I moved toward self-love. I left my husband and started working on my self-esteem and my self-love. I vowed never to put myself down again and never to let anyone else put me down either.

"I looked at the beliefs and attitudes I had about myself and started changing them to positive self-loving messages. And I eventually attracted Jimmie, a wonderful, loving man to share my life with. In other words, I got what I really wanted. It just took me about 10 years and a lot of pain in between. I could have avoided a lot of the pain and gotten what I wanted a lot faster if I would have taken a look at my own consciousness to start with."

— THE DESIRE CYCLE —

Let's go back to the question of where desire comes from. Most of you would say that it comes from inside of you, but we've already learned that deep inside we are made up of a magnificent energy source. So could it be that the wonderful energy source inside us creates desires that are specifically designed to fit the areas of our lives where our true energy is being blocked by false beliefs?

If this is a big giant university designed to strip off our false beliefs, wouldn't that make sense? Could it be that this energy source creates the desire within us and then very lovingly oversees the lessons until our desire is fulfilled? Most of our desires, when you get to the core of them, are about some form of our true nature. We want love or we want abundance or wealth. We want freedom or fulfillment. So the Universe births within us a desire and specifically chooses an area where we are carrying around false beliefs. Then lessons are specifically designed to get us to take a look at those false beliefs and change them. When the energy in our consciousness equals our desire, then it is fulfilled. We call this the desire cycle.

Can you see yet how life is all about learning and creating? We are going to say the same things now in a slightly different way and it may scare you or stimulate anger in you. Don't worry about your feelings right now, just think about these concepts and see if they might be at work in your life.

— YOU HAVE WHAT YOU WANT —

Every moment of your life, you have the people and circumstances in your life that the energy in your consciousness has attracted or created. Every moment of your life you are manifesting outwardly what you have created inwardly. Every moment of your life you are responsible for creating your own consciousness, your own energy. Therefore, every moment of your life you have in your life exactly what you want in your life!

That's the way the energy of the world is set up. You always get what you really want in your life. That's a tough one, isn't it? Even if you've come all this way with us and are open to the concept of your consciousness attracting like energy, it becomes very personal when you think of what's in your life now and you realize that you want it to be that way.

Remember, too, that we are not necessarily saying that you consciously want it to be that way. You see, every time you deposited a thought or impression in your mind, or allowed a thought or impression to be deposited subconsciously, it was still your choice. No one can make you think or do anything. You are the only one who is responsible for what is contained in your consciousness. Therefore, you ultimately choose and are choosing every moment what kind of energy you want in your consciousness.

— THE POWER OF DESIRE —

The power to express or create in an outward physical form what you inwardly desire is a natural function of being a human being. We all have the power to do this. How? It all starts with desire. Desire helps us to focus our power. The sun is very powerful but it will not make a blade of grass catch fire. However, it will make that blade of grass catch fire if we focus its power by using a magnifying glass. It's the same with our power inside. Our desires not only motivate us to learn but also act like the magnifying glass and focus our power.

We are all constantly creating and attracting the very things we desire in a physical form. We do this without even being conscious that we are doing it. Producing in physical form what we want is a natural ability just like singing. Some of us are better at it than others. And just like you can improve your singing talents by learning a few principles, so can you improve your skills at manifesting. In later chapters, we will talk about some practical "how-to's" to improve your skills at producing in your life what you desire.

Some people think that need is what manifests. They think that if they need something badly enough, God will come along and rescue them. But look around you. If need was all that it took to manifest our desires in physical form, then there would be no poverty, no homelessness and no hunger. Desire is where our power lies. Desire is what manifests.

One reason many people doubt that they have the power to create in physical form what they inwardly desire is because their lives don't always look like they consciously want them to. On a conscious level we all want our lives to be about love, abundance, peace, power, excellence, fulfillment and all the other adjectives that fit our core nature. But we have hidden false beliefs that block our energy from attracting all those same adjectives into our lives.

— THE ESSENCE OF YOUR DESIRE — (confusing)

Another reason that many people doubt that they have the power to produce what they want in their lives is because they become attached to form. The truth is that you have the power to manifest in a physical form the essence of everything you desire. Notice that we said essence. You do not have the power to manifest every physical form that you desire, but you do have the power to manifest its essence. In order to manufacture it in your life, you must distill your desires down to their essence and separate them from any form.

For example, if you want more fulfillment in your work life and you attach your energy on getting one particular job, you may not be able to produce the results that you want. You may think that you don't have the power to manifest your desires out in physical form, but the problem is not that you don't have the power, the problem is that you are attached to getting that desire manifested in a certain way. But if your desire is for fulfillment and you stay unattached to what form it will take, it will definitely appear!

If you look at your life, you will probably see many examples of this. Jimmie's daughter Alecia drove around for several years in a car she inherited from her grandmother. This car was not air-conditioned and in most people's terms, it would have been called a junk heap. Alecia happily drove this car, but all the while she desired to have a nicer car. This was probably the biggest desire she had consistently over that several year period. She finally got a job that allowed her the financial cushion she needed to be able to buy a car. For months she looked for a one or two year old used car to buy, but she was attached to having only a certain brand and style of car. After months of looking and much frustration, she reached a point where she let go of the idea of having only that specific kind of car. The next morning a similar type of car was in the newspaper for sale and it had everything she wanted and more. She bought the car and was ecstatic about her purchase.

You see, Alecia was blocking her desire to have a nice car because she was attached to having a certain kind of car. Once she let go of that attachment, the essence of her desire was free to manifest. The point is that desires from deep within us come bubbling to the surface and we quite often add form to the desire which will keep it from being manifested. The essence of your desires will manifest easily and naturally because it focuses your power or your energy outward to the physical world and attracts a like energy. But if you color that essence by trying to control what is being manifested, it may block the entire manifestation process.

— ATTACHMENT CREATES PAIN —

Some people become attached to getting what they want on a certain schedule or timetable. The truth is that the laws of energy where manifestation is concerned may work slowly, or they may work quickly. And many times, we are blocked from getting what we want because we are not ready for it yet. We may have some lessons we need to learn first. We first met back in the late-seventies, but we didn't get together as a couple until the late-eighties. As we look back now, we are so thankful that we didn't manifest a love relationship with each other during those early years. Barbara had much to learn about self-love, and Jimmie had much to learn about giving and being in a balanced relationship. We are both convinced that if we had gotten together earlier, we might have destroyed rather than enhanced one another, and we are also convinced that we wouldn't be together today.

While we are on the subject of attachment, let us say that some people, when they learn about creating their own lives and the power they have to create outwardly what they desire inwardly, become drunk with their own power. They start thinking that they can have power over everything and everyone. They start thinking that they can make someone love them or give them a certain job.

A word of caution here: Yes, you do have natural powers of manifesting what you desire. However, everyone has just as much power as you do because we are all made from the same energy source. And our energies are all designed to work in harmony with one another. You do have the power to manifest the essence of what you desire, but you don't have the power to manifest a particular form. You may get your desire fulfilled in the form that you want and you may not.

— BELIEFS OF LIMITATION —

That brings up another subject. Many people do not believe that everyone can get what they desire. They believe that if some people get what they desire, then other people will have to do without. To believe this you have to believe in a limited world. To believe this you have to believe that there's not enough to go around.

Can you believe that the energy source that created the oceans, the multitude of animal and plant life, the minerals, the planets and the atmosphere, is a limited source? Can you genuinely believe that the energy source that designed the tides, your body, the birth of new life into the world, and the rotation of the earth and other planets would design a limited, and therefore imperfect, world?

Why would this source have designed everything else so perfectly, but when it came to supply and demand, there was this one big goof? Of course, that's not the way it is. We live in a totally unlimited world, and everything, including us, is infinite and unlimited. Therefore, in order for one of us to gain, no one else has to lose. It is much like driving down an open highway. There are those who want to drive slowly and others who want to drive fast, but there's room for all of us to get what we want without anyone being injured, hurt or left out. We can all get what we want at the same time because we don't all want the same things at the same time and because we live in an unlimited Universe.

— KNOWING WHAT YOU WANT —

Now back to desires. Different people have different problems with desires. One of the most common problems we have noticed is that some people don't seem to know what they want. If you ask them what they want, they will either tell you they don't want anything or they don't know what they want. They may have been traumatized in childhood and may have a hard time feeling anything, including feeling what it feels like to have a desire or a passion. Other people have become so adept at taking on the desires of other people and suppressing their own desires that they have lost the ability to know what it is they desire.

Jimmie is a good example of this: "I spent most of my life never allowing myself to have any desires. I didn't think I was worthy of having my own desires. I was always trying to find out what other people wanted me to do so that I could do that and then maybe they would love me. Over time, I began to work on loving myself and slowly my desires began to come out."

The point is that you do indeed have desires within you whether you know what they are or not. And it's important to discover your own desires because they are unique to you. Desires bring focus, power and motivation to your life's learning process. It's important for you to experience your own desires and not just tag along on someone else's learning experience. If you follow someone else's desires, you will experience the specific learning plan that The Universe has laid out for them, not you. You and your desires are unique and so are the lessons you need to learn.

One thing you can do if you don't know what you want or don't feel like you have any desires is to start small. When you go shopping, make yourself have preferences. Try on some new styles and ask yourself if you like them or not. If the question pops up in your mind, will Mom like it or will my girlfriend or anyone else like it, put that out of your mind. This is totally about your preferences. Constantly ask yourself about your preferences. "How do I want to spend this afternoon?" "What movie do I want to see?" "What kinds of cars do I like?" "What colors?" You get the idea. The point is to start showing yourself that you do have preferences and therefore desires. You do want your life to look one way as opposed to another.

Another exercise you can do to bring up what you really want is to get quiet and still. Close your eyes and slow your breathing. Quiet your conscious mind. Now ask yourself three times in a row: "What do I want?" You may hear the answers in your head or get pictures in your mind, and if you do this often enough, you will focus on what it is you desire.

If your desires seem to be stuck, there is another exercise you can use. Find someone that you really trust. Make sure that you won't be embarrassed by anything you might say in front of this person. Also make sure that this person will agree not to judge anything you might say. Sit across from your partner and ask them to rapid fire the same question to you over and over again: "What do you want?" Tell them to be insistent with you. Tell them not to allow you to think. Your thinking may be blocking your desires. You may be editing your desires. Let them continue asking you this over and over without stopping until you finally blurt out something without thinking. What you blurted out is what you desire.

If you still can't seem to figure out what your desires are, try this exercise. Get very quiet and slow your breathing. Imagine that a doctor has told you that you have six months to live. Ask yourself a series of questions. "How would I like to spend these last six months?" "Would I live my life any differently?" "Would I be married?" "Would I be married to the same person I am married to now?" "Would I be rich?" "Would I keep this job or would I have a different career?" You get the idea. Ask yourself questions until you have covered all the areas of your life. See where you would make changes if you only had six months to live. These are your desires.

— JUDGING YOUR DESIRES —

Another problem that arises when we talk about desires is the fact that most people judge their desires. And most of us do it before it ever gets to the conscious level. We have been brought up in a society that puts everything in right and wrong categories. We are told by our parents, our churches, and society in general what a good desire is and what a bad desire is.

For instance, if you had the desire to go work for Mother Theresa, most people in our society would approve of that desire. They would label it as a good or acceptable desire. But if you had a desire to go rob a bank, most people would label that as a bad or unacceptable desire. The problem is that no desire is either good or bad. It is simply a desire. You could have very selfish motives for wanting to work with Mother Theresa. Conversely, if you found yourself wanting to rob a bank, the essence of your desire could be about wanting more abundance in your life, which is not a bad thing. Of course, the energy of robbing is an energy of lack and you would never get abundance by doing this. But the point to understand here is that the desire is not wrong or bad. You may be attached to a harmful form, but the desire and its essence are not bad or wrong. The problem for most of us is that we are so ingrained with this system of goodness and badness that we would never allow ourselves to really admit even to ourselves that we had this "bad" desire. We only allow "good" or "acceptable" desires to surface within us.

Sometimes we even judge our desires consciously and have a conversation with ourselves in our own head about how wrong our desires are. It goes something like this. "Boy, I really wish I could marry a rich man. No, I can't wish that. I have to marry for love not money. I don't want to be thought of as a gold digger. And everyone says you can't be happy if you marry for money. Well, I guess I'll just wish I was married." The problem with this is that we are judging our natural desires. Judgment will always separate you from your desires. Judging your desires will just keep you from learning more about yourself and the energy that is stored in your consciousness. And judging your desires will keep you from getting what you really want.

Oftentimes, the thing that we think we desire is not really what we desire. That's why it's important to distill what you want down to its essence. The way to discover the essence of your desire is to get quiet within yourself and ask yourself why you really want that desire. Ask yourself what will be added to your life by having this desire fulfilled. Keep asking yourself these kinds of questions until you come up with an answer that matches one of the adjectives of your pure core nature. This is the essence of your desire.

For example, a woman may start having a desire to have an affair. The essence of this desire might really be about her wanting more of the love and attention she deserves from her mate. If she judges this desire, and doesn't allow it to surface, she will just keep herself from getting that love and attention. If she allows the desire and traces it back to its essence, she will have a better chance of getting what she really wants: more love and attention from her mate.

Or a man might start having a desire to harm someone and that desire might really be about him wanting to feel more of his natural state of power. By not judging his desire, he may find some healthy ways of bringing out his natural state of power. The point is not to judge your desires, but to learn from them. You will probably be much better off too if you don't act upon your desires immediately. Give yourself a chance to find out what your desires are really about. Find the essence of your desires because that will always lead you back to your pure, core nature.

You may ask at this point, "What if I desire something that is harmful to me?" If you are honest with yourself about your desires and you desire something that is harmful to you, because of your natural powers of manifestation, you may get it. But you will learn from the experience. What will you learn? You will possibly learn about the false belief that attracted you to something harmful in the first place. You will possibly learn about the hidden energy within yourself that attracted a harmful situation to yourself. Most importantly, you will learn not to desire that same kind of energy or harmful situation anymore.

Most of the time when we desire something harmful to ourselves, we are attached to a form. If the desire is traced back to its essence, it will be about love, freedom, unlimitedness, or one of the other adjectives that describes your true nature. So again, it's important to trace your desire back to its essence and to be open to any and all forms that the manifestation may take.

— SELF-LIMITATIONS —

Another way we judge our desires is that we limit ourselves. We take on the beliefs of our parents, friends, peers or society. Those beliefs tell us that some things are possible and other things aren't. It's another way that we judge and then suppress our natural desires before they even get born. The truth is that you were made from unlimited, infinite energy and if you have the desire within you to do something, you will have the ability to achieve it. You wouldn't have the desire otherwise.

We have come to tears many times as we have been inspired by people around the world that acknowledge their desires and dare to try to express them outwardly in the world. Many of these people are surrounded by judgment from all sides, yet they still go after what it is they desire. Just imagine for yourself the myriad of different paths that are created by recognizing a desire and expressing it or suppressing a desire altogether because of your own, or someone else's, judgment. Don't let someone else's limited consciousness limit your dreams.

There are really no rules on how to live your life or what to desire. There are as many combinations of this as there are people in the world. If you will just be honest with yourself, your desires will lead the way.

JUDGMENT

*We've included this chapter on judgment after the chapter on desire
because getting what you desire in life relates back in some way
to your level of self-love. You must have enough self-love
to be able to receive what it is that you want.
Your energy of self-love must match the energy of receiving your desire.
And the single most important thing you can do to raise your level
of self-love is to remove judgment from your life.*

— RIGHT/WRONG —

Before we go any further, let's define what we mean by judgment. Webster's defines it as criticism. We think that definition is a little too nebulous because what is criticism to one person may not seem that way to another. We are going to define judgment for our purposes as anything you think, say or do that puts other people or parts of other people (their looks, actions, decisions, etc.) into right and wrong categories. Just so you'll recognize it, generally judgment puts you in the right category and someone else in the wrong category.

How can removing judgment from your life raise your level of self-love? The answer is because you can't judge someone else and not be judging yourself. It's impossible. Whatever ruler or measuring device you use for others, you will also use on yourself. Whatever you judge as good or bad in others, you will also judge as good or bad in yourself. If you have, say, a beauty standard, where you judge Elizabeth Taylor as beautiful and a woman you saw on the street yesterday as ugly, then you will also see that same beauty standard on yourself. You will judge yourself for every part of yourself that doesn't meet up to your beauty standards. You will judge yourself for every part of yourself that doesn't match Elizabeth Taylor's beauty. Or maybe you have a success standard. You judge yourself to be successful because you make a certain amount of money and you judge everyone who makes less money than you as unsuccessful. What will happen when you lose your job? You will judge yourself as unsuccessful. It will be automatic because you have a ruler inside of you that says making less than a certain amount of money makes you unsuccessful. And even if you never lose your job, you will always feel pressure within yourself to make that certain amount of money or else you'll feel unsuccessful.

— SELF-JUDGMENT —

It is impossible to judge someone else without judging yourself. Your judgment of others is simply an extension of your judgment of yourself. And when you judge yourself, you will put out an energy that is the opposite of self-love, because self-love is based on an energy of self-acceptance. The more you judge, the less you will end up loving yourself.

Whenever you judge another person, you are saying to yourself that there is something wrong with that person or that another person can make wrong decisions or do bad actions. Since we are all humans, if you see that there can be something wrong with someone else, then that also means that there can be something wrong with you. If you think that another person can make wrong decisions or do bad actions, that means that you can too. Judging others and therefore yourself says, "there can be something wrong with me" and "I can be wrong or bad". The "can be" soon turns in to "is". The more you judge others, the more you start saying to yourself, "there is something wrong with me" and "I am wrong or bad". And it will be harder and harder for you to love yourself the more you think there is something wrong with you.

Whenever you judge others you are judging the same energy that you are made of. You are made from a wondrous energy source and so is everyone else. We are all made of the same energy. When you judge that energy, which is you, you are saying that the energy is wrong to express itself like that. You are judging the very energy that makes up your very being. You are judging yourself.

— JUDGMENT ALWAYS SEPARATES —

Judgment always separates. If you don't believe that then watch what happens when a parent judges a child or a friend judges a friend. Families and friendships have long been torn apart by judgment. As a self-protective act, we always pull away from anything or anyone that judges us. We separate ourselves from the source of judgment. Whenever you judge yourself, you will separate yourself from who you really are. You will put up an invisible wall within yourself that will keep you from ever living or expressing the way you were naturally intended to. You will be out of touch with the part of you that wants to naturally express in its own unique way.

When you judge others about a particular action, trait or issue, you will often find yourself facing the same circumstances that the other person had to go through. Let's say you have been judging your aunt because she is a hypochondriac and six months later you have very mysterious physical symptoms that keep you physically disabled, yet no diagnosis is able to be found. The Universe may be trying to teach you about your own judgment. The very thing that you judge others for may soon be a circumstance in your own life.

So, if judgment is so harmful to us, then why do we do it? This goes back to the question we raised in the first chapter about why it is so threatening to us for another human being to be different than us. If we were all walking around solely absorbed in the pure love energy we were created with, without all of the false beliefs piled on top, things might be different.

If we could look inside ourselves and see nothing but the pure love, abundance, peace, etc. energy that we started with, we might be celebrating all of our differences. But somewhere along the line most of us picked up a false belief about ourselves. We started thinking we were not worthy, or beautiful. We started thinking there is something wrong with us. We started feeling insecure about our particular expression here on the earth. We started feeling weak rather than powerful, stressed rather than at peace, ugly instead of beautiful, partial rather than whole and not good enough instead of excellent.

Whatever false belief formed within us, we then tried to make ourselves feel better by criticizing or judging someone else. If we can make comparisons and we rig it so that we always end up in the right category and someone else in the wrong category, it seems to make us feel better. This particularly seems to work well for us if we are insecure about our physical expression. If I can say that brown eyes are ugly, it seems to make me feel better about having blue eyes. If I can say that brown skin is bad, it seems to make me feel better about being lighter skinned. It also works for actions. If I can say that someone who works as a prostitute is bad, and I don't work as a prostitute, then I can seemingly feel better about myself. If I can say that someone who eats red meat is wrong, and I am a vegetarian, then I can seemingly feel better about myself.

— HIDING FROM OURSELF —

Another reason we judge others is because it takes the focus off of us. We are so afraid of looking inside ourselves that we will do almost anything to keep from taking a look at ourselves or having others take a look. So we throw the spotlight on other people (their looks, their habits, their actions, their religion, anything!) so that we don't have to shine the spotlight on ourselves. And in some weird way, we feel like if we can "fix" other people, then it makes us somehow better. We believe, of course, that the way to "fix" other people is by first pointing out what is wrong with them.

The problem is that this system of judging others doesn't work. Judging will never really make you love yourself more or feel more worth. It will only give that illusion for the moment. Actually, judging others does the opposite. It will make you love yourself less or feel less worthy and will keep you trapped in an energy that is about non-self-acceptance. Worst of all, this system of judging others just perpetuates itself. The more you judge others, the worse you feel about yourself because you are also judging yourself. The worse you feel about yourself, the more you will be tempted to use the illusion of judging others to try to make yourself feel better about yourself. It is a cycle that is destructive to us all. If we are ever to have real peace on our earth, we must all work to get rid of the false beliefs that limit our love and acceptance of ourselves and subsequently our love for all of humanity.

You may think that you can judge someone and no one will ever know. But when you judge someone else, they will feel it at some level. You may be saying one thing with your words and thinking judgmental thoughts, but that person will at some level pick up the energy of those thoughts. An example of this is your boss. If you are complimentary to your boss' face but behind her back you criticize her, your boss will receive this energy at some level and it will affect your relationship. Your boss may not be able to put her finger on it, but may just have vague feelings of mistrust and of not wanting to be around you.

Jimmie used to judge an employee because he felt she was incompetent and therefore not supportive of his efforts in the overall direction of the organization. He would find himself complimenting her in an effort to motivate her and could tell that she always had a bad reaction to the compliments. Eventually she told him that she felt he was insincere, and it hit him like a ton of bricks. He realized that he had been judging himself as being incompetent in his new job and he was trying to fix himself vicariously through "fixing" her.

One thing you see in our society are people that feel that we need judgment in order to change the world. They feel very righteous and justified in judging others. For example, let's say that you feel strongly about giving love back to the earth and you see someone littering a beautiful beach and you judge that person for littering. You say to yourself, "Isn't that person just terrible for littering that way?" Do you really think that in some way it serves the earth for you to put out an energy of judgment to another human? Of course not, the way to change the world is to change your own consciousness.

Judgment can't change anyone else's consciousness, it can only change your own level of self-love and separate you from others. Just think what the world would be like if everyone changed their consciousness concerning the level of love energy we give towards the earth. There would be no pollution, no global warming and no environmental garbage. So if you want to work on changing the world, first change yourself. The example of your consciousness will do a lot to change how other people think, believe and act. If you want to do more, then educate people, without judgment, as to why it serves them to change their own consciousness concerning a certain issue. Pass along information to others who you think may be ready to hear it.

— CELEBRITY WORSHIP —

Another phenomenon in our society is celebrity worship. This is just judgment in reverse. If you see one person as better than others, you are still judging. You are saying that you are not good enough or not as good as someone else. It still places people in good/bad, right/wrong categories. Sometimes the worship of celebrities not only affects how you see yourself but other people as well. Let's say you are a male and you worship Cindy Crawford. When your wife or girlfriend doesn't measure up to Cindy's cover girl standards, you will judge your wife or girlfriend's "lack of beauty" at some level. At some level your wife or girlfriend will feel this judgment, and this kind of judgment will only serve to lower her level of self-love. As a result she may not take very good care of herself and may outwardly express this in her physical being.

It serves us to recognize and admire talent and beauty in celebrities as long as we recognize and admire talent and beauty in us all. Acknowledge that we all have talent and beauty. Celebrities are just more well known for theirs. But just because society hasn't given its stamp of approval on someone's poetry, music, acting, appearance, writing, directing, etc. doesn't mean that there's anything wrong with that expression. Honor and respect what celebrities do. Honor and respect what all people do. Honor and respect what you do.

Celebrity worship allows people to live vicariously through another person. The problem with this is that your own pure energy at your core wants to take you to incredible heights of creativity and expression. As long as you focus only on what others do, the less you will open up to your own creativity and expression from within.

Another thing you see relating to celebrities and sometimes you even see it in families is the way we put people on pedestals only to delight in tearing them down. You see many examples of this in our tabloid television shows and magazines. We love to see the "dirt" on famous people and why is this? Again, it's a way of us trying to feel better about ourselves. If we can find out that so-and-so had a nose job or has a weight problem, then we can feel better about our own appearance. We may even be able to blame our lack of success on the fact that we didn't have a nose job like she did. Or we can excuse our own lack of discipline because some celebrity has a weight problem.

You can also see this in families where one person in the family has had phenomenal financial success and when bankruptcy hits, everyone outwardly acts with concern but inwardly they are rejoicing.

There is also a form of victimism in celebrity worship. It says, "I am not responsible for my own success. If I can just get the formula from a celebrity of the 17 things they do all day, then maybe I will be successful too." This makes success and fulfillment seem like an arbitrary commodity that is granted to a few "lucky" people. It seems like if you can copy what those people do, you will get "lucky" too. It makes it seem like success and fulfillment come from outside of yourself. It makes it seem like you are not responsible for what is currently happening in your life. It's just another way of fooling yourself. Your own consciousness is the creator of your success and fulfillment, and the best formula that exists is the unique, creative expression that naturally bubbles up out of you.

Our victimism is also what makes us demand that celebrities "give back". We want them to be involved in charities and give a lot of their money to various causes. We don't seem to care if they are coming from an overflowing heart or whether they even want to give. This is just an energy of victimism which says that celebrities owe us something back because they were "lucky" enough to have something given to them.

The truth is that each person in this world attracts their own financial and professional success and they don't owe anyone else or The Universe anything back. The Universe is unlimited and when someone attracts energy in the form of fame or money, it does not have to be replaced. One of the most beautiful things successful and famous people do is to show the rest of us, just by their very being, that our dreams are possible.

— EMBARRASSMENT SEMINAR —

We raised another question in our first chapter about why we in our society find it so hard to be different from the crowd. We all want to fit in, be cool, be normal, and be part of the group. When we were in Hawaii for the first time together, we decided to play a game that we called our embarrassment seminar. The game was for us to notice when either of us was being embarrassed about something. We easily hit 50 times before the week was up. Of course, we ended up laughing a lot. But what was really surprising and not so funny to us was how we shut ourselves down and held ourselves back, even if it was just for a moment or in very minor ways, because of the fear of disapproval by someone else. It was our own judgment of ourselves that separated us from really being ourselves.

When we try to be like everyone else, it creates an energy of distrust of ourselves. It says in subtle ways that our unique expression is not good enough or not right because it is not normal. The paradox is that as we fall in sync with everyone else, we may be keeping ourselves from being in sync with our own self. Anytime you are out of sync with your own self there is, at the very least, uncomfortableness and at the worst, pain.

Many of us have seen individuals who have kept a secret about themselves for years and been in pain. They have been living a lie by suppressing their natural instincts and trying to look normal or appear to be like the masses. When they finally let the secret out and accepted their unique expression, they were much happier and more comfortable with themselves. The point is that we are all unique in our human expression and our consciousnesses are also unique. We will all have less pain if we accept our uniqueness and allow it to be expressed. Only then will we be able to accept the uniqueness of others.

— LABELS —

This is probably a good place to talk about labels. Our society seems to be fascinated with labeling, categorizing or stereotyping human beings. We label our gender, race, age, astrological sign, profession or no profession, part of the country we hail from, habits, diseases, political beliefs, religion, hobbies, physical appearance, and manner of dressing, just to name a few. If we truly are unique in our expression, then why do we lump all smokers, Southerners, alcoholics, blondes, Baptists, men, Capricorns, women and Asians in the same pot?

The truth is that labels can be dangerous because they remove your uniqueness. The more you label yourself, or allow others to label you, the less unique you will appear to be. You will take on the energy of what you and others think and believe about that particular label. If you label yourself as a Southerner, then you will take on the energy of what you and other people believe a Southerner is like. You will act and think like you and others think a Southerner should act and think. You will see the world only through the eyes of a Southerner. And most importantly, you may deny some of your natural instincts that don't match up to the way a Southerner "should" act or think.

We have all been brought up with these labels and most of us have accepted them without question. In fact, to most of us, the labels have felt good. Labels seemed to give us a sense of identity or a place to belong. The problem is that, before the labels, we already had an identity, a very unique and beautiful one. This goes back to the false beliefs and insecurity we talked about earlier. Labeling ourselves is just another way of trying to fit in because we are afraid that our particular expression isn't good enough. We are afraid of the very energy inside of us. If we can find someone else to identify with, it seems to make us feel less insecure about our own expression. But along with labels come the false beliefs and limitations that either you or society or the group being labeled have attached to them.

It's obvious to see how labels deemed by society as negative will limit you. Try wearing a label of criminal, old person, fat person, alcoholic, or poor person. It's easy to see how these labels might limit you in this world. Labels will limit you, even if you only take on the ones that our society calls positive ones. Let's say you identify with the label of athlete. The problem is that you are so much more than just an athlete. You are much more than a beauty queen, philanthropist, doctor, young person, boss, leader or rock star. You are a magnificent, unique expression that is too wondrous to label.

Labels also separate us from other humans. If I call myself a Baptist, it obviously separates me from Catholics. If I call myself a smoker, it will separate me from non-smokers. If I call myself a Southerner, I will carry energy in my consciousness that separates me from Northerners. The problem with this separating energy is that for all of us, our natural state is harmony with other human beings. We are related to each other by our divinity and our humanity much more than any label could ever unite us.

One of the more stupid labels we wear is race. If you study anthropology and trace all races thousands of years back to their true origins, you find that all of what we now call races started from the same place. If you look around today, you'll see fair skinned people with large lips and slanted eyes, brown skinned people with straight hair and blue eyes, and golden skinned people with curly hair and large noses. There are no features that "belong" with a certain skin color. Race is just another label someone thought up somewhere along the line that helped them feel better about their own physical expression. Race is just a label that someone used to judge others and therefore rationalize their destructive behavior towards others. The truth is that there is really only one race, the human race, and any sub-headings under that are just labels that some of our more unhealthy forefathers thought up.

— YOUR OWN UNIQUE EXPRESSION —

So dare, if you will, to start seeing the world through your own unique expression and through your own unique consciousness. Dare to get rid of the labels you have carried with you for years. Dare to see the world, not through the eyes of your parents, your priest, your boss, your friends, your community or society in general. Dare to see the world as the perfect, unique, unequaled, singular expression that you are. Think for yourself and resist taking on labels. Instead of describing yourself as a Southerner, try describing yourself as a beautiful human being who happened to be born in a Southern town. And most of all, dare to see yourself as one who is too wondrous to label.

— NOTICE DIFFERENCES WITHOUT LABELING —

Sometimes we judge another person's outward appearance or expression without ever bothering to get to know that person. We put labels on them and have them all sized up and judged before they ever get within ten feet of us. If you find that you do this and you'd like to stop, we have an exercise you might want to try. Actually it's more like a game. You can play it at any public place where you will be around people that you don't know.

To play the game, just notice all the differences in people, without labeling or judging them, like you are watching fish in an aquarium. Delight in those differences and each person's unique right to express those differences. See each person as having a right, perfect and beautiful physical expression. Resist any attempts to label anyone or criticize their physical being. Instead, send out any encouraging, uplifting, appreciative thoughts that you want. Instead of thinking, "Look, there's another redhead," think, "I'll bet that woman loves having such beautiful red hair." Instead of saying, "Ugh, look at that punk with the spiked hair," think, "Wow, isn't it great that that person has enough guts to express themselves that way with their hairstyle?"

Pick out what you think are beautiful, unique features in everyone. Don't skip anyone. See it as a game and the game is that everyone has unique beauty, and it is your job to find that beauty. Over time, what will happen is that this game will have a profound effect on your consciousness. It will expand your appreciation of the unique ways that humans express themselves and vastly change your definition of the word beautiful. You will truly start to see everyone as beautiful, and it will help you to admire your own beauty. And it may expand your ideas about new ways to express your own uniqueness.

— UNDERSTANDING —

Another thing you can do to banish judgment from your life is to try to gain understanding. If you understand where a person has been and what they have been through, it helps you to refrain from judging them. Think about how many times you've been on a highway and you're driving about 65 m.p.h. and you come up on someone doing 25 m.p.h. You let out a string of expletives and maybe even hand gestures until you get up next to that car and see that the person's car is going as fast as it can go. Instantly, your anger and judgment are replaced by understanding.

Being gentle and understanding with other humans is very similar. Realize that most human beings are only doing the best that they can do. Realize also that most human beings are only doing what they think they need to do to take care of themselves. A woman dances in a strip club because that is what she thinks she needs to do to take care of herself. A man deals drugs because that is what he thinks he needs to do to take care of himself. Realize that how someone looks or what they do is not wrong, it may just be different from you. Realize that judgment from you will not help these people learn, grow or change. Your judgment will only separate them from you and push you both farther from the truth. Create an attitude of understanding within yourself. It will help to create a better understanding of yourself and it will increase your own level of self-love.

Just remember, you never know what someone else is going through or has been through. Barbara can remember after the three children died and she had been physically very sick, she would encounter someone's criticism and judgment. She was so beaten down that she just wanted to scream at the person and say, "You just don't know what I have been through or you wouldn't be talking to me like that". It didn't matter if they were just critiquing her outfit, she was in such incredible pain that any little vibration of judgment was more than she could handle.

— QUIETLY PRESENT WITHOUT JUDGMENT —

The Universe is a vast web of connected energy. Nowhere in that energy is there a vibration of judgment. The energy of the Universe is just quietly present, everywhere, always moving toward Its own expression. The Universe doesn't judge. It just keeps quietly expressing Itself as you and everyone else. It would serve us all if we would use the Universe as our model. If we would all be just quietly present without judgment, allowing the flow of our core expression and delighting in that same flow from others, the energy of our life would be miraculous.

Uncovering the Iceberg

By now, you have become aware of the fact that you probably have many false beliefs, thoughts, feelings and impressions which help to make up your consciousness. And these beliefs, thoughts, feelings and impressions all carry with them a certain kind of energy which attracts outwardly into your life a like energy. Some of them may be things you want to change, and we'll talk about how-to's in a future chapter. But this chapter is about discovering the energy you are carrying around in your own consciousness.

There is a part of your consciousness that you are conscious or aware of already. You have beliefs, thoughts, opinions, attitudes, feelings, and impressions that you already know about yourself. But, just like the iceberg analogy, there are parts of yourself that are hidden. You are not consciously aware of what these parts are. And just like the iceberg, the hidden part may be the larger of the two parts.

We have already discussed the fact that you will learn, whether or not you become conscious of the false beliefs. The Universe has set it up so

that everyone learns. Your learning just becomes easier, less painful and
quicker if you make a decision to become more self-aware and start
uncovering the iceberg.

— SELF-AWARENESS —

The whole process of becoming more self-aware is a process of questioning and noticing the thoughts, feelings and actions in your life. The best way to start the process is to become like a "fly on the wall" in your own life. Or you may prefer to think of yourself as a photographer who videotapes your life and then plays it back. Or you may feel more comfortable playing the role of a reporter who reports objectively back to you concerning your life.

The trick is to notice and not attach judgment, shame, or embarrassment to anything you see. Noticing is a lot different than judging. You can notice that you didn't like the way you handled a situation and want to do it differently next time. This is very different from mentally or verbally beating up on yourself for the way you handled a situation. Noticing is different than judging. You can notice that you still have "poverty messages" playing in your mind or actions that put out an energy of lack. This is different than judging yourself for having that kind of energy in your consciousness. The point is to be gentle with yourself. Remember that this is a learning process with the emphasis on process. If you had nothing left to learn, you probably wouldn't still be here. The goal is not perfection. The goal is to keep learning more and more about yourself.

This is not to say that when other people are involved and your words or actions have hurt others that you should not make restitution or apologize. You still don't have to judge yourself while doing this. You can just realize that you would like to have handled the situation differently and then do so next time.

— INNER RESISTANCE —

As you learn more about yourself, you may encounter resistance within yourself. A lot of us still strive for perfection rather than learning, and we tend to resist learning about ourselves because it exposes our imperfections. We are so attached to being perfect that we'd rather hold on to our perfection than to learn the truth about ourselves. If this occurs, gently remind yourself that the goal is learning, not perfection. And if you've made a commitment to self-awareness, recall that commitment to mind.

This is not the easiest or the most pleasant part of getting what you want out of life. This is the part where you will find out things about yourself that you may have kept hidden for years. You may find things in your consciousness that outright disgust you. You may even experience anger or shame. We do promise you, however, that whatever vile, disgusting or defeating things you find along this pathway, that you can change them and therefore change your life.

You may be disappointed that you only see the energy that you would like to change, after the fact. In other words, only after you have thought the thought or done the action are you able to see the energy that you are putting out. Don't let this discourage you. If you are at least recognizing different types of energy that you are putting out, it means you are close to making changes and getting what you want.

— QUESTIONING YOURSELF —

To go through this process of uncovering the energy in your consciousness, essentially what you will be doing is questioning yourself. You will be asking yourself questions about why you acted a certain way or had a certain kind of thought. You will be digging deeply in your consciousness until you get down to the level of your beliefs. This questioning may be painful, but it is not nearly as painful and dangerous as not questioning.

Think how many tragedies in history have occurred because men and women complacently acted without questioning themselves or society or anyone else. The most intense examples we can think of are Hitler and slavery. Think how different history might have been if each soldier in Hitler's army had questioned himself about what he was doing. Think how different the history of the United States would have been if men and women questioned slavery. Not to question is much more painful and dangerous for us as individuals and as a society.

— PATTERNS —

To start your quest, take a look at your life as it is now and work backwards from there to learn about yourself. What patterns do you see? First, take the areas that are causing you the most pain or unhappiness in your life. Look for repetitive patterns. Let's take an example to get you started. We have a female friend who always attracts and gets involved with unavailable men. To her, it just looks like her life is a series of twisted circumstances in which she is a victim. She has dated a married man that "can't" get a divorce, a man who "doesn't want commitment," and a workaholic who travels all the time.

It is probably much easier for her to blame the wife, or the mother, or the overly demanding boss. Instead, she could take a look at the pattern in her relationships and she might be able to discover that she is the one afraid of commitment or intimacy. She might discover that she has a false belief deep down that she's not worthy of having a man's love. It could be a lot of things. Only she can know what her false belief is about. The point is that if she continues to unconsciously go about her life as a victim, sort of in a cloud of self-delusion, she will continue to attract people and circumstances with the same kind of energy as the false belief.

We can't give you examples of all the patterns in the world. We can only get you started in this process. We'll list several areas for you to take a look at. You don't have to use one of our examples because we want you to choose the area you are most unhappy with first. But you might want to read through some of the following questions. Perhaps you'll get an idea of the type of questions you can ask yourself to uncover patterns in your life.

RELATIONSHIPS

What are the patterns you see? Do all the people you have had relationships with have any traits in common? Do you see a common thread in the way you have been treated in these relationships? How about the way you have treated the other person? Do you tend to have the same kind of trouble with all of your relationships? Do you end the relationship or does the other person? Do you have a pattern of leaving or not leaving? Do you have patterns in your life that keep you from getting into relationships?

MONEY

What are the patterns you see? Do you constantly feel like there's never enough? Is there more than one area of your life where money is a problem to you? Have you ever had these kinds of problems before? What kinds of feelings come up for you when you spend money? Are your feelings different when you spend money on yourself than when you spend money on others? What kinds of feelings come up for you when you pay your bills? How does your work fit in to your concept of money? How does having or not having money make you feel?

WORK

What are the patterns you see? Do you constantly have co-workers that you can't seem to get along with or don't like? Do you seem to have the same types of problems with different people at work? Do you hate or like your work? Have you always felt this way? Have you ever been happy at work? When? Have you advanced in your career as much as you thought you should? Has this always been the case?

Once you have discovered some patterns in your life, you have made a giant, empowering step. By simply discovering the patterns in your life, you have started uncovering the iceberg of your consciousness. You have started mapping out its blueprint. Whenever there is a painful pattern, there is also a false belief. Behind the painful pattern in your life, you have a belief that is not about abundance, love, fullness, beauty, health, freedom, power, excellence, fulfillment, unlimitedness, intelligence and harmony. The next step is to uncover and free yourself from these false beliefs and then you'll be on your way to getting what you want out of life.

— DISTILL FALSE BELIEFS —

To learn about the kind of energy you are putting out you should distill your false belief down to its essence or its deepest reasoning. To help you identify what a false belief looks like or sounds like, let us tell you that false beliefs when traced down to their essence will be about lack, limitedness, hate, indifference, insecurity, not being whole, ugliness, powerlessness, unfulfillment, disharmony, fear or some adjective that closely resembles one we've listed here. The way to get down to your deepest reasoning is the same process for getting to the heart of your desires. Ask yourself questions.

This process of asking yourself questions is very similar to other processes we have previously covered. First, get your mind and body quiet. Then take a pattern that you have discovered and ask yourself what false belief is behind this pattern. Ask yourself what part you have been playing in attracting or allowing these circumstances or people in your life. Don't judge the process or have a timetable expectation for the answers. Don't require that the answer has to come in any certain way. It may come to you right then as a thought, or an image, or the answer may come to you seemingly out of nowhere as you go about your day. It may even come in a dream. Simply know that you will get the answers to your questions because the answers are already inside of you. If you truly want to know the answers, they will come to you.

— PRESENT CIRCUMSTANCES —

After patterns, you should take a look at specific circumstances that you find yourself in now. What is it you don't like about your situation? What situational patterns did you discover that relate to this circumstance? What is it you want to change? Do you want more money, or more love, or a better job?

The first step is to take responsibility for what is in your life now. Admit to yourself that you participated in attracting, allowing or actively seeking out the current circumstances of your life. Realize that the energy of the current circumstance exactly matches the energy of your consciousness. Ask yourself what false belief may be behind this circumstance. Ask yourself what belief you may be holding on to that is not about love, abundance, fullness, beauty, health, freedom, power, excellence, fulfillment, unlimitedness and harmony. Ask yourself why you attracted each situation, each event, each pattern.

— PEOPLE IN YOUR LIFE —

After you have finished with the circumstances in your life you should go through the same process with the people that are in your life. Start with the relationships you are most unhappy with and ask yourself how you may be contributing to your own unhappiness. Ask yourself what false belief you may be holding on to that is blocking you from getting the love you want.

The answers may come immediately or they may take some time. Some people take a very analytical approach to this and others take very casual approaches. Although there is no right or wrong way, we do suggest that you don't make the process hard by adding tension and worry to the process. An attitude of quiet confidence along with an open mind and some quiet time will go a long way towards finding your answers. All of the answers you will ever need are already inside of you. Allow those answers to surface, and they will.

— ACTIONS AND THOUGHTS —

In our quest to be perfect, we sometimes rationalize away our patterns or blame someone else for our circumstances. That's why we suggest that you don't stop your questioning there. It is much harder to rationalize away your actions and your thoughts. That's why taking a look at them is the next and most important step in the process. Your actions and your thoughts are the biggest signposts to the kinds of false beliefs that are stored in your consciousness. When your patterns and circumstances don't uncover the false beliefs, take a look at your actions and your thoughts. Sometimes you can fool yourself or rationalize away your circumstances and the people in your life. But thoughts and actions, unless you are consciously trying to change the energy, will be amazingly consistent with the energy that is contained in your consciousness.

Start with an area you are unhappy with. Let's say it's one where you've already discovered some patterns, but you are having trouble figuring out what false belief is behind those patterns. Take a look at your present day actions and compare them to what you consciously think about yourself concerning that particular area of your life. Compare your actions to what you think your beliefs are about that area of your life. Look for the places where your actions differ from what you think you believe. For this you will have to become a very good observer of yourself.

Let's say that you have been using affirmations and think you believe in your natural abundance. If we were to question you about the things you think you believe, we might get answers like this: "I think I deserve abundance. I think the abundance of the Universe is mine. I think the abundance of the earth is unlimited." Now, at this point you've already uncovered your patterns of never having enough money, so you know that there's a false belief in your consciousness somewhere. So take a look at your actions. You may find that you cheat on your taxes, never spend money on yourself, or always try to get your friends to pay the lion's share of the restaurant or taxi bills. You may have figured out a way to get the local cafeteria to give you a free cup of coffee by hiding your coffee cup while in line. You may go shopping and never get out of the sales racks. Do these actions seem consistent with what you thought was in your consciousness? They probably do not.

Now, trace each action back to what kind of energy it's about. Cheating on your taxes is probably coming from an energy of lack. You think there is not enough money so you have to cheat. Never spending money on yourself is probably about a belief that you are not worthy. You get the idea. Take a look at the actions in your life and see what kind of energy they are about. The energy you find in your actions is also the kind of energy that your false belief is about. And you will keep attracting this same kind of energy back into your life so it's important to be honest with yourself here.

— ENERGY BEHIND ACTION —

Be careful not to assume that any given action carries with it a certain kind of energy. It's not the action itself, but the energy behind it, that you are trying to discover. For instance, society tells you that it's good to be nice. But if your niceness is stemming from a lack of self-love or fear of what people think of you, then that may not be an energy that serves you. So make sure that you look behind the action to discover what kind of energy is really there.

You can do the same thing with the thoughts in your life. Let's examine the thoughts that might run through your head all day. Let's say you had the following thoughts: "Grrr. Look at those people in that Cadillac. Rich people make me sick." "She can't win this Bingo game, I wanted to win more than she did." "I can't afford that." "I'm never going to get ahead."

— ENERGY BEHIND THOUGHT —

Now, take a look at the energy behind these thoughts. The thought about the rich people in the Cadillac and the one about the Bingo game may be about a belief in limitedness. You may think that if someone else is rich, it will keep you from being rich. But that would be coming from an energy of limitedness, and that false belief may block you from your own unlimited abundance.

So, if what you want is more abundance in your life, then you will also have to get to the point of wanting abundance for everyone else who also has that as a desire. Otherwise, you will be coming from limitedness and that energy will return limitedness back to you. The thought about not being able to afford something and the one about never getting ahead were probably coming from an energy of non-abundance. In other words, for some reason, you truly don't believe that your natural state is abundance, or you don't believe that you will ever see it in your life. This kind of negative, non-abundant energy will return non-abundance back to your life.

— READ YOUR ENERGY —

The point is to be aware of what you think and what you do. Read the energy of your actions and your thoughts. They will tell you a lot about the false beliefs inside of you.

There is no way that we can help you read the energy of every situation in your life, but we can talk about several different types of energy. By the end of the chapter, you should have learned enough about the art of reading energy to apply it to your own situations.

— ENERGY OF FEAR —

Let's start with fear because every false belief relates back in some way to the energy of fear. The energy of fear or worry will always attract the very thing you are afraid of. This is because whatever kind of energy you focus on consistently becomes a belief. And remember that whatever kind of energy you broadcast from your inward beliefs will be balanced by a like energy outwardly in your life.

So fear thoughts will cause you to focus your energy consistently until the fear becomes a belief. That belief will attract a person or situation with a like energy, and you will attract the very thing you are afraid of.

This is an energy principle that we have seen played out in our lives many times. Barbara remembers her mom constantly being afraid that she or someone else in the family would get hepatitis. She made an incredibly big deal out of making sure that everyone washed their hands all the time in order to avoid hepatitis. Every time she asked them to wash their hands, she would say, "Wash up, because you might get hepatitis." Guess which person in the family ended up with hepatitis? You guessed it, Barbara's mom.

Jimmie at one time owned a real estate company with about 40 employees. He was constantly in fear that his salespeople would leave his company and go with another company. His every action and thought centered around trying to keep that from happening. In the end, he attracted the very thing he was most afraid of and all of his salespeople left. If Jimmie had been able to look at his thoughts and actions back then, he would have seen that everything he was doing and thinking was all based on the energy of fear.

We would like to mention here that every fear thought does carry the energy of fear. However, as we talked about before, an isolated thought doesn't carry the same intensity of energy as does a thought that is laid down over and over again until it becomes a belief. So we don't want anyone to get scared about having isolated thoughts of fear. Yes, an isolated thought may carry fear energy, but an isolated fear thought by itself, unless it has other like energy in your consciousness to align with, doesn't have enough energy by itself to attract the thing feared.

It is the buildup of fear thoughts and actions over time that create the kind of fear energy that will attract the very thing you are afraid of. The beliefs you have deep inside, that come from an energy of fear, are the ones you will want to work on changing. And if you do discover an energy of fear, we don't want you to worry about that either. Remember, earlier we said to notice, not judge. And here it is important to learn about yourself without getting down about what you learn. Focus your energy on what you want, not on what your false beliefs are.

— ENERGY OF CONTROL —

It is also important here to let you know that most actions and thoughts that are about control are generally rooted in the same energy as fear. If you find that you are always trying to control other people and/or your circumstances, then you probably have the energy of fear at the core of your consciousness. For instance, if you try to control what your spouse wears in public, this is probably related to a fear of your spouse looking attractive or not looking attractive enough. This could indicate a fear of losing your spouse or a fear of what other people will think about you.

— ENERGY OF JEALOUSY —

Behind jealousy you will usually find the energy of fear or sometimes you will find the energy of limitedness. When you are jealous because your spouse is talking to an attractive person of the opposite sex at a party, that kind of energy, if you trace it back, is about fear. You are afraid of losing your spouse, or maybe you are afraid of your spouse being too good for you. In either case, it is important to find out what is the false belief behind the fear so that you can change it.

If you are jealous because your best friend gets a great new job, the energy behind jealousy in this case is about limitedness. You have a false belief that there are not enough good jobs to go around.

— LOVE OR FEAR —

If you find the energy of fear in your life, it will always be about a false belief. Your natural energy is about love which is expansive and unlimited. The energy of fear is always about contractedness and limitedness. Love will always feel like love; fear feels anywhere from gross, brutal abuse to highly subtle disguises that even resemble love. That's why it is important for you to recognize fear and search beyond it to find out what false belief is behind it. It is important to discover which of your beliefs are about contractedness or limitedness.

The first step in doing this is to admit that you are afraid. Don't run from fear. It will only increase. Realize that fear is not there to hurt you. It is only there to help you see your false beliefs. Fear wants you to see the reality of who you really are inside. Fear wants you to let go of your illusions. Fear is only a teacher. Fear wants to lead you to expansiveness and unlimitedness. Once you understand why fear is there, and get rid of the false belief, the fear will disappear from your life. So, if you find yourself uncovering fear in your life at this point, make sure that you let it teach you. Ask it why it is in your life. Ask it what it has to show you about your consciousness. It is never the intention of The Universe for us to continue to live in fear. It is only there for a season to teach us about ourselves.

So if you find fear in your life, look beyond it to find the false belief underneath. It might be easy to see or you may have to dig through several layers. For example, it may be easy for you to see that your fear of losing your mate may be about your lack of self-love. Or your fear of not being in control may be about a false belief that you are not free in the first place. And your fear of what other people think of you may be about your lack of self-love. But it may be harder for you to see that your jealousy about other men's attention towards your wife may be not only because you are afraid of losing her, but underneath that fear may also be the false belief that you are not worthy of her or that you have something wrong with you or that you are not a whole person without her.

Distill the fear to its deepest essence then you will know what you really have to work on. Knowing the truth about yourself is always the first step in getting what you want. Old patterns will begin to fall away as you remove from the foundation of your consciousness the false beliefs that have been there for so long.

— ENERGY OF HIDING —

Another energy you may want to learn about is the energy of hiding or running away. If you notice thoughts or actions within yourself with this kind of energy, just know that when you hide or run away from something, it will increase. For instance, if there's something painful or unpleasant in your life, and you run away from it or hide from it, the situation will only get more painful or more unpleasant.

When Barbara split from her second husband, she didn't take anything material. She gave him the house and the car. However, she didn't take care of herself because her name was still on the mortgage note for the house. Several months after she moved out, her ex-husband quit paying the notes. She didn't find this out until three years later. By this time, the bank was foreclosing and seeking the sheriff's fees, the back notes and lawyer's fees from her. Instead of dealing with the people at the bank, Barbara freaked. She tried to avoid getting served with legal papers. She asked friends not to tell the sheriff where to find her. The end result is that even now, ten years later, Barbara's credit is not in good shape because of this incident. If she had contacted the people at the bank, she might have been able to work out some sort of settlement or payment plan. The energy of running away or hiding always makes a situation worse.

Jimmie has a similar financial situation. In a previous marriage, he didn't have money one year to pay for his taxes so he, and his wife at that time, just didn't pay them. They avoided the tax man for several years, and when the I.R.S. finally caught up with them about three years later, they not only owed for back taxes, but also penalties and interest which amounted to almost double what they owed in the first place. If they had just faced the situation, instead of running from it for three years, they could have avoided a lot of the penalties and interest.

— ENERGY OF PROCRASTINATION —

It is also worth noting here that the energy of procrastination is generally the same kind of energy as running away or hiding. Procrastination may make you feel better for the moment, but the pain of the situation you are avoiding will generally increase in proportion to the amount of time you spend procrastinating.

— ENERGY OF CHEATING OR STEALING —

The energy of cheating or stealing is almost always about lack. There is some false belief inside of you that believes you are less than abundant. If you were abundant, you would never have to cheat or steal from anyone. The worst part is that cheating or stealing from someone else will only create more lack in your life. The same energy you are putting out will return to you. Even if you steal in secret and no one knows that you cheated or stole, the energy will be there and it will attract more lack into your life.

Only take what is freely given to you by the Universe. If there is any doubt that something is freely given to you, then it probably has a cheating or stealing energy surrounding it. Think about some of the small ways that you may be keeping yourself in lack. You may be cheating on your taxes or your expense report at work. You may be skimming a few dollars from the cash register at work now and then. You may be trying to get a store to charge you a lower price by hiding the correct price tag or saying the item came off of a sales rack when it didn't. You might hide an expensive item as you go through customs so you don't have to pay duty on it. All of this kind of energy will bring more lack, less money, and less of your natural abundance into your life.

For some, stealing is about power. Stealing from another person makes them feel powerful. The problem with this is that they usually have to use some kind of weapon or attack only when they are in a gang. This will only bring more powerlessness. Each time they use a weapon, they are telling themselves that they are not powerful in and of themselves. They are telling themselves that they only have power when they have a knife or a gun. Each time they attack as a gang, they are telling themselves that they are not powerful on their own. They are telling themselves that they are only powerful when they have their gang members with them. This only perpetuates the false belief of powerlessness and blocks their natural state of power.

— ENERGY OF ABUSING —

Now, let's take a look at the energy of abusing or intentionally hurting another person. The one thing an abuser doesn't usually realize is that he/she can't see him/herself one way and other people another way. You can't value something in yourself and not value it in others or vice versa. Therefore, not to value other's privacy, physical body, emotions, sexuality, individuality, dignity, life, or intelligence is not to value your own. If you invalidate or suppress someone else's emotions, then you probably don't value your own emotions. You can't put out energy that takes away the dignity of another person and have respect for your own dignity at the same time. In other words, the way you treat others speaks volumes about the way you see and treat yourself.

Of course, abusing someone or putting out intentional hurt will also attract abuse back to yourself. And it will also keep you in pain because harmony, not hurtfulness, is your natural state. Anytime you are not in alignment with your natural, core energy there will be pain somewhere.

Abuse is a vicious cycle for an abuser. By abusing someone else, the abuser is trying to value him/herself in some way. They may be seeking more power, love or respect, but in some way they are trying to value themselves more. But an abuser will never raise his/her own value by abusing someone else because each time they abuse someone else, they are mirroring back to themselves their own lack of value. They aren't valuing other's privacy, emotions, sexuality, etc. and this mirrors back to them their own lack of value for their own privacy, emotions, sexuality, etc. The worst part is that they can sometimes get caught in this cycle of trying to raise their own value by continually abusing others.

The people that get abused by others also get caught in a trap. Any time abuse happens, it makes the abused person see themselves with a little less value. Some psychologists might say that it lowers the self-image. The less you value yourself, the more you set yourself up to attract further abuse. If you value yourself less, you will be putting out an energy to the world that says "I am not worthy" and you will attract an energy that exactly matches your own devalued view of yourself.

This may be why people who are abused usually don't just get abused by one person. They continue on in their lives and attract many abusers until they change their perception of their own value. And unless and until they realize what they're doing and change their thoughts and actions, the cycle will continue and the pain may even get greater. This is why it is so important that as adults, we make sure that we support, encourage, and edify children rather than tear down, suppress and abuse them. Abuse is an action whose energy carries with it very long term effects.

People who are abused can also get caught in the trap of abusing others because they don't value themselves, and therefore, don't value others so they may try to abuse others to try to raise their own value. Of course, as we say above, this doesn't work. The only way to escape the cycle of being abused or being an abuser is to get rid of your own false beliefs and work on loving and valuing yourself.

— ENERGY OF LYING —

The energy of lying or hiding the truth is oftentimes a futile action because, at some level, other people are picking up the truth. At some level, everyone knows the truth no matter how convincing you may be. Also, at some level, people will not trust you because they know the truth, and then because they don't fully trust you, other people may hold themselves back from being totally straight with you.

People who are used to being totally honest won't like the feeling they get from being around you, and you will begin to attract only those people who are also into lying. So, if you put out dishonesty, you will also attract it into your life. You should also know that the Universe will always move towards exposing the truth, because Its very nature is only about truth. So if you are lying or hiding the truth, don't be surprised if you find circumstances cropping up in your life that expose the truth.

Lying or covering up the truth about yourself is also an energy that will perpetuate non-self-love. Each time you lie about yourself, you are telling yourself that there's something wrong with you. Your energy is saying, "Why can't I just be me? Why do I have to cover up who I am by lying?" Lying about yourself is an energy of apologizing for who you are.

Lying always has some fear energy tagging along with it because if you lie, you are always afraid that the truth will be exposed. When you lie over a period of time, you will hold this contracted energy of fear in your body, mind and emotions. We all know that stress is now linked to all kinds of disease. Imagine what holding this kind of tense, contracted energy inward will do to your body, mind and emotions? We can only liken it to taking a long drag from a cigarette and holding it in your lungs for several years. Imagine the damage that it could do. Holding on to fear energy over a period of time is like keeping yourself in constant stress.

It is easy to see why people lie in our society. They lie because we judge them. A woman is afraid to tell her parents that she is pregnant because of their judgmental reaction. A man is afraid to tell his girlfriend that he wears a hairpiece because he is afraid of her disapproval. If you find that you are attracting people in your life that are hiding the truth from you, first take a look at how truthful you are being with others. Next, take a look at how judgmental you may be of others. If you want the truth from others, weed out judgment from your life. And remember, you won't be able to stop judging other people until you stop judging yourself.

— ENERGY OF DEPENDENCY —

The energy of taking care of another adult person on the surface seems like a loving energy. However, if you totally take care of another person, how is that person ever going to learn about his or her own power? How will that person learn that they can take care of themselves? The energy of totally taking care of another adult person takes that person's power away from them. It makes them powerless. The energy of helping someone get back on their feet may be a very loving energy. And the energy of teaching someone about their own power to take care of themselves may be a loving energy. But an extended period of too much giving of your energy can create an energy of powerlessness in another person. It says, "I am powerful because I can help you, but you are powerless because you need my help."

You can't be powerful and totally dependent at the same time. That's why independence feels so good. It reflects your natural power back to you and outward to the world. No one can tell you how long a period should be of helping someone get back on their feet. Just know, that to totally take care of a capable adult for an extended time period can rob them of their natural state of power.

Many of our government programs have been designed to rob people of their natural power. We have set up long term programs to totally take care of many people who are capable of taking care of themselves. It is no wonder that so many people who have been caught up in this system are also caught up in an energy of powerlessness. Long term programs that encourage people to find their own uniqueness and express it and short term programs that help people get back on their feet would be much more helpful to them in the long run.

Oftentimes, when you learn to read the energy in your life, you will come up against values that you learned from parents, teachers, religious leaders or society in general. You must be careful not to label energy as good or bad, just because that is what you were taught.

— GIVING OR TAKING —

For instance, in our society, the act of giving is thought to be loving energy. What you must do in reading your energy is look behind your actions into your beliefs and motivations. The act of giving can be a very beautiful, loving energy. But it can also be a taking energy. For example, a lot of what is called giving energy in our society is, in truth, people giving of themselves in order to feel better about themselves.

A person who volunteers their time to help raise money for charity could be giving out of a pure love energy. But this could also be someone who has a low level of self-love who needs this act of giving to charity in order to feel better about him/herself. This is really an energy of taking because the person wants something back in return; they want to feel better about who they are as a person.

Jimmie used to send birthday cards to all of his relatives and even acquaintances. When he would meet someone, he'd inquire about their birthday and then follow it up later with a card on the celebrated day. The problem with this is that Jimmie realized later in life that he was only sending out these cards because he wanted everybody to think he was a "good" or "nice" person. He wasn't just giving out all of this energy because he wanted to. He wasn't just overflowing with love and spilling it out to others. He was giving to others so that they would like him. What he was really doing was sending out a taking energy because he wanted love and admiration back from those to whom he "gave". And what this kind of "giving" out to others was telling his consciousness was that he was not enough in and of himself. He was telling himself that others wouldn't like him if he was just himself. With these acts of "giving" he was telling himself that he needed this persona of "nice person" in order for other people to like him.

— DOING VERSUS BEING —

Sometimes people "do", so they don't have to "be". In other words, sometimes people give and do for others so that they can hide behind this persona of "nice person" and they don't have to take a look at what kind of energy is really inside them. They are so scared of taking a look inside that they would rather just put on a "nice" persona so that neither they nor anyone else will take a look at their true energy.

When giving energy is pure love energy, it wants nothing back in return. When you are giving out of a pure love energy, you naturally want to give. It almost hurts not to give. You are so full of love, abundance, peace, fulfillment, etc. that you want to give some of it to others. You won't be able to help it. It's not something you have to strain or try to do. When you are full, giving is the most natural thing in the world.

— GIVING AND RECEIVING —

So the next time you give out energy to someone, if you find that you are intent on getting a thank you or a high feeling from the act of giving, then chances are that you may be giving but wanting something in return. In other words, you may be putting out a taking energy. It would be better for you to give to yourself first. That is why the first step in learning to give is learning to receive. When you have sufficiently received and you are full of self-love, giving out love energy will be natural and unforced. It will be like the ebb and flow of the ocean. It will only flow one way so long and then it reverses to flow the other way. You can only give to yourself so much until the flow will naturally reverse and you will give out to others.

— ENERGY OF SELFISHNESS —

Since we're talking about giving and receiving, you might ask at this point, what about selfishness? What is the energy of selfishness about? A selfish person is a person who never really learned how to receive. They think that they have to take everything. They are generally hiding a false belief about lack, limitation and non self love. Selfishness is a different kind of energy than that put out by a person who is learning to give to themselves and receive what is divinely and rightfully theirs. Giving to yourself out of an energy of self-love is one of the highest forms of energy. It will guide you through the process of learning to receive and end you up at fullness and learning to give to others. Selfishness will only teach you about taking energy which is about lack, limitation and non self love.

— ENERGY OF RESCUING —

What about the energy of rescuing someone else? We live in a physical world where there may be physical consequences for a person's thoughts and actions. These physical consequences are not there to cause suffering. They are there for us to learn from. If you take away someone's consequences, you take away the vehicle that is there to teach them. No matter how well intentioned you might think you are being, you may be blocking someone's learning by removing their consequences. That person may need the pain of those consequences in order to learn a particular lesson.

A common example would be of a teenager who's irresponsible behavior gets him kicked out of a private school and his parents rescue him by getting him admitted to another private school. And when he wrecks his car because he was drunk, they buy him a new one. The consequences of this teenager's irresponsibility will just keep getting bigger and bigger until they are so big that the parents can no longer rescue him from them, such as a jail sentence.

What they are teaching the teenager by continually rescuing him is that there are no consequences for irresponsibility. The problem with teaching that is that it goes against the natural energy of what irresponsibility says. Irresponsibility says, "I want less of this in my life," and the energy of irresponsibility is not going to change. Irresponsibility will continue to attract less and less of people, situations and possessions for this teenager until he learns about its energy and changes his behavior. By removing his consequences, his parents are removing his learning.

— RESCUER CONSEQUENCES —

Now, let's take a look at the other side of rescuing someone. Let's take a look at taking on consequences that are not yours and how that kind of energy impacts your consciousness. Usually taking on the consequences of another person takes something away from you. It may be your time, your money, your privacy, your freedom, or anything else valuable to you. When you take on someone else's consequences it says to you that you (your time, your money, your privacy, etc.) are not as important as the other person. It devalues you. This is always an energy that is the opposite of loving yourself. So by rescuing, you not only are not really helping the other person, you are also lowering your own level of self-love.

— BALANCE OF GIVING AND LEARNING —

Some of you could argue, then, that since we all attract everything in our lives, then it doesn't serve us to help or give to anyone.

If a person is poor, some would say that they need to feel the consequences of being poor so that they will learn about their abundant nature. And if a person is sick, then we need to let them feel their pain of sickness so they will discover their own energy of health.

What you may not realize is that some people on this earth are not capable of learning in their present circumstances. If a person is hungry or doesn't have a roof over their head, how is that person going to focus on learning who they really are? And if a person is focused on a debilitating disease, how can that person be expected to focus on anything else?

The point is that a person may not be physically, mentally or emotionally able to learn at different times in their lives. One of the most compassionate things we can do is to help to create an environment for all people that is conducive to learning.

If a person is hungry, he must be fed before he can learn. And if a person is sick, we might be able to relieve pain or ease some worry so that the person is more able to tune in to their learning. There is a fine line or a balance, if you will, of giving without taking a person's power away. There is a fine balance of giving out to others without blocking their learning. And there is a beautiful kind of giving that gives from an overflowing heart to create an environment that is conducive to all people's learning. We call that kind of giving, loving someone back into their own natural truth.

— ENERGY OF SYMPATHY, EMPATHY AND COMPASSION —

This might be a good time to talk about the energy of sympathy, empathy and compassion. The energy of sympathy focuses on the powerlessness of a person. It says, "poor you". The energy of empathy focuses on both your powerlessness and that of another person. It says, "poor us". The energy of compassion feels the pain of another person and yet focuses on the divine energy within that person. It says, "I am so sorry you are having to go through this but I know you have the power within you to get through it". Oftentimes, compassionate energy will offer, "tell me how I can help you to help yourself". And oftentimes, people just need to have their feelings heard, they don't really need to have someone say "poor you or poor us".

We must be gentle with one another for we are all here for the same reason, to learn. Use any energy you have overflowing within you to help another person uncover the beautiful energy within them. Our actions of giving to others are important, but the greatest thing you can do is to uncover your own natural energies because if everyone loved themselves enough to do this, we'd have quite a beautiful world.

We have given you many examples of reading energy, but the list of situations is endless. The point here is just to watch yourself and discern what kind of energy is really behind your actions, your thoughts, the people and circumstances you attract into your life.

Ask yourself constantly, "What am I really telling myself by this action?" "What kind of energy surrounds that thought?" If you are honest with yourself, you can use this knowledge to change your consciousness and start getting what you really want out of life.

PRACTICAL HOW-TO'S

Besides removing judgment from your life,
the most important thing you can do to bring yourself closer
to realizing your dream is to get rid of any false beliefs that relate
to the dream. Let's say that you want more money in your life
and you have discovered that you have a false belief
that there's not enough to go around. You realize that you have
false beliefs relating to lack and limitedness. The most important
and significant thing that you can do to attract more money in
to your life is to get rid of these false beliefs and allow your beliefs
to center around your natural abundance.

— MASTER OF YOUR ENERGY —

So, how do you get rid of this energy of your false beliefs once you have uncovered them? You can't destroy it because we know from science that energy can't be created or destroyed but you don't have to carry it around with you either. Realize that you are the master of your own energy. You are the one who gets to make the decisions about the kind of energy that circulates in and around you. If there is energy in your consciousness that you don't like, then send it elsewhere and allow your pure natural energies to surface.

— POWER OF TRUTH —

Also, realize that the energy of truth is much more powerful than the energy of falseness. Why? Because anything having to do with the truth aligns you with your true nature. Anytime you are aligned with your true nature of love, abundance, fullness, beauty, health, freedom, power, intelligence, excellence, fulfillment, unlimitedness and harmony you will be more powerful than when you are aligned with any false beliefs or illusions, no matter how powerful they may seem. Anything having to do with the truth is the exact opposite energy of the falsehoods or illusions.

Therefore, truthful thoughts, feelings, impressions and actions will easily, over time, cancel out, change, or transform the energy of any false beliefs that now reside in your consciousness. So, in order to change the false beliefs in your consciousness to the truth, you must change your thoughts and actions to align with that truth. Changing your thoughts will change your feelings and, over time, will help to form new beliefs. Changing your actions will also help you to form new beliefs. We sometimes say that actions speak louder than words, and that is also true with your consciousness. Sometimes the energy of what you do speaks louder or impacts your consciousness more than what you say.

In fact, if you will watch how you live your life the odds are that you may be thinking one thing yet acting in a different way. Your thoughts and actions are not in alignment. You may find, if you watch how you live your life, that it is quite easy to think one way yet much harder to act that way.

For example, it's so much easier to say you will stick to a diet, quit drinking caffeine or quit smoking than it is to actually stick to what you think or say. You may find more subtle examples in your life. But the most subtle examples will probably relate to the innermost issues that you are consciously, or even subconsciously, working on in your life. You may find yourself thinking about changing your behavior in some way over an extended time period yet you keep acting in the same old way.

— ALIGN THOUGHTS AND ACTIONS —

That's why it is important to work on changing both your thoughts and your actions simultaneously. If you consciously think truthful thoughts, but allow yourself to act in a manner that is inconsistent with the truthful thoughts, it will be harder for your consciousness to decide which one you really want. On the other hand, if you change your actions to be in alignment with your true nature, but you still allow negative, false thoughts to reign in your mind, your consciousness will again be confused as to what belief you really want to keep and what belief you want to get rid of.

For example, if you have discovered that you have a false belief that you are stupid and you really would like to get rid of that belief, you might start by changing your thoughts concerning your level of intelligence. You might start consciously thinking thoughts that positively reflect on your natural, divine intelligence. You might stop telling yourself derogatory remarks, either aloud or in your head, about your level of intelligence and replace those with positive messages. You might, at the same time, start reading books or playing games that previously you thought were too hard for your intellectual level. If you worked on your thoughts alone or your actions alone, your progress would not be as swift. You need to act and think in a way that is the opposite of the false belief. In order to change your beliefs from false ones to the truth, you need the combination of acting and thinking that is consistent with the truth.

— CHANGE YOUR THOUGHTS —

So, the question arises, how do I change my thoughts? The first step is for you to realize that you are the master of your mind. Your mind is just like a giant computer and you are responsible for what goes in and what comes out. Just like a computer, if you feed it negative, false, unhealthy thoughts, that's exactly what you'll get back. But you do have the power to change what you put into your mind. You do have the power to change your thoughts. But over time, you may have fed your mind with a lot of negative, false, unhealthy thoughts so you have to expect when you are first starting to change, that you will have a lot of negative, false, unhealthy thoughts come up. Don't resist them. Don't fight them. You will only make them seem as though they have power. They don't. You are the one with the power.

Whenever you have a thought come in to your mind that is not consistent with what you want, simply change the thought that very moment to one of positive, truthful, healthy energy. Whenever you have thoughts come into your mind that you don't want, simply choose to think thoughts of truth instead. Let's take a look again at the example we used earlier with the person who wants to stop believing they are stupid. When the thought arises that says, "You are so stupid", what that person needs to do is change that thought to an opposite, truthful, positive, healthy thought like, "I am blessed with natural divine intelligence". Over time this will help to change their belief that they are stupid.

Sometimes you may find that you have a false belief that is very stubborn. It keeps coming up in your thoughts and actions and you can't seem to get rid of it. First realize that this is a process and it took you many years of compiling this energy in your consciousness so it may take some time to get rid of it as well. A technique that might also help is for you to trace the energy back to where you think it came from. Figure out who or what the source of this false belief was. Then, when it comes up in your thoughts or actions again, mentally give that energy back to its source.

For instance, let's say that you were raised with a sibling that always made fun of your appearance and told you constantly how ugly you were. Now, as an adult, you still have thoughts and actions that agree with that false energy. When the thoughts or actions start to come up, mentally give that "ugly" energy back to your sibling. Tell the energy to go back where it came from. That energy did not originate from you. You started with an energy that is about beauty. Then affirm the kind of energy you want in your life. Tell your natural, beautiful energy at your core that you want it to surface. Make mental statements to yourself about what kind of energy you want in your thoughts and actions concerning your appearance. Since you are the master of your own energy, the energy must obey and, over time, you will be able to get rid of even the most stubborn of false beliefs.

— CHANGE YOUR ACTIONS —

To change your actions, you must first discover what self-defeating actions are in your life in the first place. As you begin this process of self-awareness, you may not uncover all of the actions that are sabotaging you at one time. The more time you spend in introspection, the more things you will discover in your life that are inconsistent with what you really want. Another point to remember is that you may not be able to immediately or fully change everything you uncover.

For instance, if you want more money in your life and you discover that always buying sale items seems to you like you are giving off an energy that is inconsistent with your natural state of abundance. You may not currently have the financial resources to stop buying sale items, but you can at least buy maybe one item a month that is not on sale. And when you do buy items on sale, you can tell yourself that you are choosing to buy sale items but you aren't compelled to buy sale items. After all, very wealthy people sometimes choose to buy sale items.

It seems like this would be an appropriate place to mention that no one can read your energy except you, and you can't read other people's energy either. An action or thought may be inconsistent with one person's desire or dream, but it may be totally consistent for another person. Or one person may be learning their lessons very quickly and moving on in their process rapidly, making rapid, major changes in their lives, whereas another person with the same type of desire may be moving more slowly, making only minor changes.

The point is to make sure that you are only trying to read your own energy and not trying to teach, fix or change anyone else. If someone has asked for your help in reading their energy, the best thing you can do for them is to throw out some scenarios of what false beliefs may be stored in their consciousness or behind their behavior. Once uncovered, you can also suggest ways of changing beliefs, thoughts and actions, but the person involved is the only one who will know the right action to take because, after all, it's their lesson.

Another thing you can do is to talk about the past and present energy in your own life so that another person would have examples from which to learn. Just remember that the only person who can know whether an action, thought or a belief is consistent with what they really want is that person.

— PRACTICAL HOW-TO'S —

Here are some practical how-to's that will help you change your false beliefs and attract your desires. Not using these techniques won't hurt you. Using them may just help you to get what you really want more quickly and easily.

— FOCUS YOUR ATTENTION —

Get clear on exactly what it is you want and really focus your attention on the desire. Whatever you focus your power or your attention on becomes reality for you. Most people don't realize how powerful they are.

Focusing your attention on something causes it to grow and become real for you. Let your whole being know what you really want by having your desire involved in every moment of the day that you possibly can. Think thoughts and take actions that are consistent with your desire.

If you're looking for a job, focus your attention on the fact that you are going to get a great job, exactly the kind of job you want. Diverting your attention would be to focus on all the unemployed people out there, the nature of the economy or anything else that could undermine your own belief in your ability to attract an ideal job for you. If you focus on these negative thoughts, they will become a reality for you. If you focus on what you want, it will become a reality for you. Another part of focusing your attention is to take actions that are consistent with your desire for an ideal job. Don't allow your time to be squandered away with numerous other activities. Your time is a measure of what you are paying attention to and whatever you pay attention to will grow and become your reality. If you spend your time in activities that are focused on your desire, you are helping to draw that desire in to you.

Let's try an exercise to show you what we mean. Look at a painting, any painting. Focus on that painting, really focus. Notice colors, brush-strokes and details that you never noticed before. That's the same kind of focus you need for whatever you desire. That kind of focus says very clearly, and very powerfully, "this is what I want." It sends a message to all of your inner beliefs to get in alignment with this singular desire.

— ZERO IN —

Zero in on only one thing at a time. Having a whole bunch of desires swirling around in your consciousness will only serve to dissipate your energy and will dilute your powers of manifestation.

Focus on your major desire. Place all of your energy on your one, most important, heart's desire and you will attract that desire much quicker. Once you've attracted a desire like that, you will be even more motivated to continue manifesting in the same manner, and you will have built a strong belief within yourself in your ability to attract whatever you want.

— LIVE YOUR DREAM —

Think and act now the way you would if you were already in possession of your dream. Allow yourself to imagine what it would be like if you had your dream right now. Notice how you can tell that there would be some differences within you and also outwardly in your life. Now imagine the effect you would have on your life if you lived right now like you already had your dream.

Do you see the power in living your dream, as much as you can, right now? By living your dream now, you place yourself inwardly and outwardly in the same energy of the dream. Can you see the impact that this might have on your consciousness and how it can help you attract your dream more quickly? Make changes in your life even if they are small ones that match the way you will feel and live after your dream is realized.

— AFFIRMATIONS —

Affirmations are a good way to replace false beliefs with the truth. Affirmations are just statements that you say to yourself aloud or within your own mind. Invest a few moments in yourself on a consistent basis. Find a quiet place, close your eyes, and find the quiet center within yourself. Affirm to yourself, in the quietness of your own mind or say them aloud, positive statements that relate to your desire. "I deserve a wonderful, loving relationship." "I am a wonderful, loving person". "I have all the abundance I will ever need." "I am attracting a wonderful person to share love with".

Remember to make your affirmations positive statements and avoid using words like not and never. Sometimes your mind doesn't hear the not or never so instead of "I am not fat," you might try "I am slim and beautiful." Also, make sure to talk in terms of now, not later. Instead of, "I will be employed in a wonderful job," try, "I am employed in a wonderful job." It may seem funny to you to affirm things that you don't yet see as reality in your life, but this helps you to inwardly believe in having a new job.

Remember, when the energy of your consciousness equals your desire, you will have the essence of your desire. Affirming your desire like you already have it changes your energy to equal your desire.

— VISUALIZATIONS —

Impact your consciousness with visualizations. Remember that your consciousness is like your own personal blueprint of what you want. Your consciousness is influenced, by you, every moment. Visualizing is simply using the power of your imagination to impact your consciousness. In the stillness of your own inner mind imagine yourself already in possession of your desire. Create an image, or at least a sense, of you having your desire. Imagine all five senses, if you can, being stimulated by your desire. See, feel, taste, hear and smell what it would be like if your desire was already a part of your reality.

Remember that the essence of your desire is important, not the form. So in addition to getting a clear picture, or clear sense, of all the physical details of your dream, it's also a good idea to visualize the inner characteristics of yourself as you will be after you have your desire. Feel the joy, happiness, peace, security, or love that having your desire will inspire within you. This way it'll keep you from focusing just on a particular form that may be somewhat different from the real essence of your desire. There are many books available with more information concerning affirmations and visualizations if you decide that these are comfortable and effective techniques for you.

Jimmie remembers an example where visualizations helped him realize a dream. He was the owner of a real estate firm with 16 salespeople at the time. In the history of the company, they had never collectively gotten more than 18 listings in any one month. Real estate was in a slump and the country was in a recession. During a sales meeting at the end of January, Jimmie explained the concept of visualizations to his salespeople. He then asked them to get quiet within themselves and visualize a number of listings that they felt they could personally commit to getting in the month of February. They were asked to write this number down on a piece of paper and then walk to the listing board and visualize themselves writing that number of listings on the board with a February date. Jimmie asked them to keep visualizing their goal everyday for the entire month. Collectively, they had personally committed to 30 listings. By the end of February, the company achieved 54 new listings.

— DAILY QUIET TIME —

One of the best tools for realizing your dream is to spend quiet time every day, whether in meditation, taking a long walk by yourself, taking a warm bath without distractions or any way that you choose to slow your life down. Listen to your innermost being and align with the energy that's there.

— EXPECT YOUR DREAM, WITHOUT ATTACHMENT —

Maintain within yourself an attitude of expectation that you will have your dream, yet without a controlling, needy, attached energy. The energy of expectation allows the energy of your desire to flow out and attract back to you the like energy of your desire. Controlling, attached energy stays bottled up inside of you and blocks the flow of receiving. At best, you'll attract what you're attached to which will likely be a limited version of the real essence of your dream. Unattachment is open and flowing. Attachment is contracted and constricted.

— PREPARE TO GET WHAT YOU WANT —

Put yourself in the position of receiving. To continue to live in your old established habits and patterns is to do nothing to prepare yourself to receive something new. Your old thought patterns and life style will do nothing to attract a new, loving relationship in your life if that's what you want. Look at your surroundings, how you spend your time, how you spend your money and what kinds of thoughts you think. Are they consistent with getting what you want? Do you want to be wealthy but don't know the first thing about the responsibilities involved in having wealth? Or have you thought about how you would manage your wealth and perhaps prepared yourself by doing some reading or taking a course?

— ASK FOR WHAT YOU WANT —

Put out the energy of your desire into the world by your thoughts, words and actions. We live in a physical world in a physical body, and all the inner consciousness work you can imagine won't bring you what you want unless you bring that energy out of yourself and into the world.

When Jimmie was hired by a hospital, part of his job was to attend seminars and conferences to enhance his professional growth. When the hospital was sold shortly after he was hired, a seminar trip to San Francisco was canceled because all budgets were frozen. Jimmie accepted the disappointment at first, but when the accounting department called him a few days later and said the check to pay for the conference had already been cut, he decided to ask his boss once more if he could attend this seminar. The thought occurred to him that if he didn't ask for what he wanted, he would never get it. So he ran down and told his boss about the check being cut, discussed the fact that part of his job was professional growth, and then asked if he could still go. Even though she had already told him he couldn't go, her answer this time was yes.

Countless times, we have both been traveling and had the desire to fly first class. Many times, we have had an out-of-date coupon for an upgrade or been flying with the wrong kind of fare for an upgrade, but just by asking for it, we have received the upgrade anyway. The point is to always ask for what you want.

— WRITE OUT WHAT YOU WANT —

This is yet another physical thing you can do to focus on

your desire. You are impacting your inner consciousness by focusing your thoughts and actions while writing out your desire. And you can intensify this focus by reading what you've written out on a daily basis. You can also focus your thoughts and actions by using other physical symbols of your desire. Pictures from magazines of what you want, artwork, jewelry or any other physical symbols that remind you of your desire, can also impact your consciousness because they consciously and unconsciously focus your attention on your desire. As part of the decorations of our home we have many art objects and other creative pieces that we have collected from around the world that remind us of our dreams and of our true nature.

— WATCH YOUR ENERGY —

Watch what kind of energy you consciously or unconsciously program into your consciousness. The television shows you watch, the music you listen to, the books you read and even the people you hang out with all have an impact on your consciousness. Some of it even happens unconsciously. That's why advertising works. Whatever we listen to over and over, even though it might be unconsciously, starts to be believable to us.

Also think about the music you listen to and think about how few times you have to listen to a song to know its lyrics. Now, think about those lyrics. Are those the kind of thoughts and beliefs that you want programmed in to your consciousness? When we were looking for contemporary music for our wedding reception, we had a hard time finding enough music to fill up a couple of hours. Most of it was "you broke my heart and I hate you for it" kind of stuff.

When Jimmie was looking for a job, he literally had to stop reading the newspaper and watching the news because there was nothing positive or encouraging about jobs or the economy that was being said. If he listened to what was being said on the news, he would have had an uphill battle with his own belief in his ability to attract a great job.

If you are working on loving yourself more and you want to get rid of judgment in your life, you may want to quit watching some of the talk shows or tabloid shows on television. Some of the talk shows encourage the audience to participate in judging whether a guest is right or wrong, good or bad and even encourage the audience to make decisions for the guest's life. Some of the magazines available also have very negative, though well-intentioned messages.

The point is to be aware. Think of what kinds of energy you are feeding your consciousness. Be aware of the kinds of messages you are picking up every day. Literally, everything in your life has an effect.

— MAKE A LIST OF YOUR DESIRES —

If you are having trouble believing in your power to manifest what you want in your life, one suggestion is to make a list of ten of your desires and post it where you'll see it often.

When Jimmie first did this years ago he was making a come-back in his real estate career and was going back out into the field as a salesperson instead of working in management. At the top of his list was a certain income he wanted to make for that year, which was considerably more than he had been making. Also on the list was a new car. Jimmie looked at his list daily and visualized himself already in possession of the things on his list. Around three or four months later, he suddenly realized he had received some of the smaller items on his list. This gave him confidence in his power to manifest. Shortly thereafter he got a great deal on a slightly used Volvo with which he was delighted. And then, at the end of the year, Jimmie's income went over the mark of what he wanted. In fact, it was amazingly close and exceeded his desire by only a few hundred dollars.

— BE IN MOTION —

When we first started dating, one of Barbara's favorite analogies was what Jimmie began to call her "parked car" concept. He was pretty stuck in his life at the time and got tired of hearing about the parked car so it's special to us and makes us smile to talk about it now. Barbara used to tell Jimmie that he could theorize all he wanted to, and he could meditate all day long, but unless he got out into the world and spread his energy around, it would take a long time for him to attract what he wanted into his life. And then she would inevitably get around to telling him that it was like having a parked car.

Even though it had all the potential for getting him where he wanted to go, it wouldn't do a thing for him until he got in it and drove it.

The energy of your desire is meant to be expressed. Start wherever you are now and take however tiny of a step you need to take, but trust yourself enough to begin to put your desires into motion. For instance, if your dream is to open your own business and you sit at home waiting for the right business to come along, you may wait a long time. Even if you can't quite see your way financially to start the business yet, there are many small steps you could take that would lead you closer to your dream. You could do research into different types of businesses, different types of accounting methods, different types of phone systems, or whatever you might need in running your own business. If you already know what kind of business you want to start, you might do part-time or full-time work at a similar type business to learn from it or take a course about it at a local college. The point is to get in motion toward realizing your dream.

— ALLOW YOUR EMOTIONS —

From years of public speaking, sales training and positive thinking, Jimmie used to cover up, or deny, how he really felt about something when he would encounter any kind of friction in his life. He lived in a bubble of positive thinking that covered up the reality of his life. He was not allowing any feedback from himself that may have helped him make changes for the better.

Allow yourself to feel the discouragement, the disappointment, the impatience, the frustration, the fear and the pain. Life, growth and manifestation are all a process and part of that process is uncovering the false beliefs that you have about yourself. Your emotions will teach you about your false beliefs if you will allow yourself to have them. Welcome whatever comes up for you in your life and look at it as the teacher that it is.

Disappointment is one emotion that sometimes comes up when you are going for your dream. One thing you must realize is that not getting what you want may be the first step in helping you get what you want. This is because not getting what you want will sometimes intensify your desire. And intense desire is what will manifest your dream. So allow your disappointment while at the same time realizing that this "no" you are getting now may be helping you to one day get a "yes" to your dream.

— DON'T SHARE YOUR DREAM WITH EVERYONE —

It would seem like the thing to do is to talk about your desire with all who will listen, but we have found that not to be true. If you share your desire, your beautiful unique dream, with everyone, you may get incredible amounts of negative, limited reactions back from them. Not everyone is supportive and thinks unlimitedly. All of that negative energy raining down on you may shake your own belief in your power to manifest your dream. If you are going to share your dream with someone, make sure that this person is going to be some-one who will support you in reaching that dream. Also make sure that you share it with someone who will not limit you or your dream. Treat your dream as a precious treasure. Don't allow anyone to ravage that treasure. Only share your treasure with people who are able to appreciate it and who will also see it as the precious treasure that it is.

— WEED YOUR GARDEN —

We like to use an analogy when we talk about changing the ener-gy in your consciousness. See your consciousness as a flower garden. See your false beliefs as the weeds that you want to replace with lovely flowers. Weed your garden. Replace thoughts and actions that don't serve you and your dreams with those that do. See your dreams as beautiful flowers. Use some of the techniques we've outlined here or some of your own to plant and water those flowers. Realize that every moment you're either allowing weeds to grow or you're plant-ing and nurturing beautiful flowers. Consciously choose a new direc-tion every time you notice yourself going down the same old weed-filled path. Choose new thoughts and new actions that serve you. The more you do this, the more you'll notice the weeds disappearing and a beautiful, healthy flower garden in its place.

ATTRACTING MORE LOVE
IN YOUR LIFE

Since love and abundance are two desires
that a great many people have, we are going to get more specific
about the energy of different attitudes,
ways that you may be sabotaging yourself and
specific ways to speed those desires into physical form.
This chapter is about attracting more love into your life.

— DO YOU LOVE YOURSELF? —

If you want more love in your life, the first thing you need to take a look at is how much you really love yourself. Realize that the level of love (the kind of people or no relationship at all) that you are now attracting exactly matches the energy of self-love presently in your consciousness. Whatever the level or intensity of love that you have for yourself is the kind of love that you will attract in your life. If you love yourself unconditionally, then you will attract people into your life who also love you unconditionally. The problem is that most of us don't love ourselves to that extent yet. So, how do we figure out how much we do love ourselves and increase that love energy in our lives?

— HOW DO YOU SPEND YOUR TIME? —

Again, this is a process of noticing. Notice how you spend your time. Do you do things that you love to do? Or, are you always doing what others want you to do? When you are with other people, do you honor your desires and consider them as important as anyone else's desires? How often are you spending time doing the things you love? Do you even know what it is you love to do? One exercise that can be helpful is to make a list of ten things that you truly love to do. Then, make sure that each week you do at least one activity on the list until you form a habit of always doing things that you love These can be simple things like taking a long, relaxing bubble bath or playing a round of golf. Or they can be more complex things that give you pleasure like white water rafting trips or cruises to nearby islands. Make sure to include a lot of items on your list that you can do by yourself and that are within your control. Don't sabotage yourself by convincing yourself that you can only be happy and loving to yourself by going to great parties or taking trips to Europe for which you presently don't have money.

Notice how you value your time, your possessions, your emotions, your body, your opinions, your preferences and your privacy. Anytime you allow energy that devalues these things, it is probably not an energy of love. If you are always allowing others to waste your time, that is not a very self-loving act. Let's say you have a friend who always shows up over an hour late each time you meet with him. By consistently allowing this to happen, you are putting out energy that says, "My time is not valuable." Time is truly the most valuable commodity you have been given while on this planet. Allowing someone to squander your time is not an energy of self-love. There are many ways to handle the situation which we won't go into, but the point is not to continue to allow this to happen in your life.

— YOUR POSSESSIONS —

Your possessions are an expression of your uniqueness. Anytime you don't value your possessions, you are putting yourself in an energy that is the opposite of love. If you don't care what kind of house you live in or clothes you wear, you could be stuck in an energy that is less than loving. People who love themselves surround themselves with beautiful, loving environments and adorn themselves according to their own beautiful, unique preferences.

— YOUR EMOTIONS —

If you don't value your emotions, you could be putting out an energy that is less than loving. Let's say that you don't allow yourself to be sad because other people won't like you. Or maybe you surround yourself with people that laugh at your feelings. Neither of these is loving energy toward yourself.

— YOUR BODY —

Valuing your body is also loving energy. How much time do you devote to taking care of your body? Do you abuse it with substances like food, drugs, alcohol or cigarettes? When you value your body, you give love to yourself.

— HONOR YOURSELF —

The point here is to value or honor everything about yourself. Stand up for yourself if someone devalues you in any way. Treat yourself the way someone who truly loves you unconditionally would treat you. Fall in love with yourself and treat yourself accordingly. Others will soon follow suit.

— YOUR MONEY —

How you spend your money is another indicator of the loving energy you have towards yourself. Do you always tell yourself "no" when you want to spend money on yourself? Do you find it easier to spend money on other people than you do on yourself? Spending money on yourself is important in learning to love yourself because money reflects energy that you have put out into the world. Money is the physical symbol for the energy that you have put out in your work or professional expression. If all you do is put out energy and get nothing back, that is unbalanced.

True love is never unbalanced. It flows both ways. It is important for you to say "yes" to yourself with your money. No matter what your situation, you can say "yes" to yourself occasionally and allow those occasions to grow closer and closer together. You can also get into the habit of saying "yes" to yourself with small things. Barbara used to go into a drug store when she needed to feel more love for herself, and she would tell herself that she could have anything in the store that she wanted. She knew that she couldn't do much damage to her budget in a drug store. She would end up with new lipsticks, a new color of nail polish or magazines and a bill for less than $20. But that $20 was important to her process of learning to love herself.

— LOVE AND JUDGMENT —

Since we've devoted a whole chapter to judgment, let's just say that if you are still judging other people, you are still judging yourself. If you haven't read the chapter on judgment, you may want to now. If you start delighting in other people's differences and their unique right to express themselves in any way they prefer, you will also free up your own natural expression and you will accept and love yourself more.

The judgment of other people's actions is just as harmful to your own self-love as the judgment of their physical expression. If you judge other people's decisions, and how they live their life, you are also judging yourself. Start seeing the actions people take as them doing the best that they can do. Start seeing the actions they do, not as something wrong or bad, but as something they thought they needed to do to take care of themselves.

Remember, we are in the same university and in the same process of learning who we really are. Maybe you took a course that others haven't learned yet, but then, maybe they've taken courses that you haven't learned yet either. Maybe you're strong in one area of learning that someone else is weak in, but that doesn't make you any better. If you look for them, you'll probably find areas in everyone from which you can learn.

— CHANGE YOUR PHYSICALITY —

Another way to increase your self-love is to improve or change your physical expression or your physical surroundings in any way that pleases you, makes you feel more comfortable or makes you feel better about yourself. You must realize though, that whatever action you take may not please your friends, spouse, parents, peers, family or society. You need to trust yourself and be willing to lose or gain weight, change your hair color, change your name, get an education, get a nose job, change your clothing style or move into a new part of town if it makes you feel better about yourself.

Just remember to make changes in your life only if it pleases you. You are the one who lives in your body, your apartment, your neighborhood and sleeps in your bedroom. Don't make changes in your life just to please others because that will put out an energy that is the opposite of self-love. Make changes in your body and in your life that make you happier, more comfortable or increase your self-esteem.

— ARE YOU GIVING LOVE? —

If you want to attract more love in your life, you also need to take a look at your life and see how much love you are giving out to others. The energy of giving out pure love energy will always attract back loving energy in return. Giving to others doesn't have to be giving your money or your time, although those are two good vehicles. You can give your wisdom, your knowledge, your smile, your kindness, your possessions, your support, your inspiration, your talents, your patience, or your attention, just to name a few. And you don't have to give out love just to other humans. You may choose to give love to animals or plants. You may choose to give love by being active in environmental causes that give back to the earth. The point is that love comes in many forms. Listen to your heart and you will know what is the most natural way for you to give out love energy.

— RECEIVE LOVE —

Put yourself in the position to receive love. Go to places where your desires lead you. In other words, if your desire is to meet a wealthy man, go to stockholders meetings or charity balls. If you desire to meet someone who has a love for working out or sports activities, go to health clubs or scuba or dance classes. We have a friend who wants a relationship in his life, and he has decided that the most important quality that he desires for this person to have is that she must love animals. Therefore, he is going to volunteer at the local zoo. The point is to trust your desires, and let them lead you to places and situations where you will put yourself in the position of receiving the love you want.

— LIMITED THINKING —

Don't let your thinking get limited by the limited thinking of society or by your own negative thoughts. A few common examples of the type of things you'll hear from well meaning friends and society in general are: "There aren't any straight, single men available," "All single women have children," or "There aren't any good ones left." If you listen to this kind of limited thinking, you will soon believe it. And what you believe will become your reality.

The types of things you tell yourself can be even more destructive. If you tell yourself things like "I'm so fat" or "I don't have a good body" or "I'm a failure," pretty soon you will believe those things and create that for your reality. If you want love for yourself and to create more love in your life, you must make a commitment to yourself to stop putting yourself down and stop telling yourself negative, limited, false statements. You need to replace those false, limited thoughts with positive, truthful statements about your true nature. Talk to yourself constantly about how loving, abundant, fulfilled, peaceful, etc. you are and you will soon believe it.

— TAKE RISKS —

Don't be afraid to join a club by yourself or approach someone on an elevator. If you never put out energy that says, "This is what I want," you will most likely not get it. If you truly want love in your life, you must be willing to do things that may make you uncomfortable in order to get it. The first time we kissed, Barbara leaned over in a taxicab and kissed Jimmie. She took a small risk that developed into a relationship of epic proportions.

— PREPARE YOUR LIFE —

Prepare your life for getting what you want. Look at your life. Is there room in it for a relationship? Do your friends, furniture, artwork, and lifestyle scream "single"? How about your habits that you know you will have to get rid of for a relationship to work? Maybe you are a male who has a habit of watching females as they walk by and deep inside you know that this kind of behavior will be a point of contention in any relationship. There's nothing wrong with you watching females, it's just that this kind of behavior has an energy that screams "single."

Maybe you are a female who has a shopping habit that has gotten out of hand, and you know that most men wouldn't put up with that kind of credit card debt. There's nothing wrong with spending money the way you want to spend it, but realize that in a relationship, you will need to put out energy that considers both parties, not just what you want. Make small changes in your life that prepare you for and move you toward having a love relationship in your life, and that energy will attract one for you.

— USE VISUALIZATIONS AND AFFIRMATIONS —

When you visualize, see yourself receiving love from someone. Feel the joy or passion that you desire. Hear words being said to you that you have longed to hear. Smell cologne or scents that remind you of being loved. Use all of your senses. Act and think the way you would after you have a special someone in your life. For some people, this might mean wearing sexy underwear or setting an extra place at their dinner table. Do anything that makes it seem as if you already have what it is that you desire.

— UNHEALTHY RELATIONSHIPS —

One of the hardest things to do is look at past patterns of unhealthy relationships and walk away from any relationship or pattern that seems to be in the same energy of unhealthiness. For example, if you have a history of being with controlling men and know that in the past it was hurtful to you, then an act of self-love would be to walk away from any and all relationships that also seem to have that same controlling energy.

Sometimes this can be painful because we have the capacity to fall in love with people who are not good for us. And it can also be hard because many times we tell ourselves that there won't be anyone else out there that will be any better. But if you walk away from any relationship that is less than the loving relationship you want and deserve, your self-loving energy will attract a higher level of love back into your life.

If you are currently in an abusive relationship, you must walk away from it if you are going to attract more love in your life. It is almost impossible to love yourself and be in the middle of abuse at the same time. It doesn't matter what form the abuse takes. It could be sexual, emotional, physical or mental. The longer you stay in this kind of relationship, the less you will end up loving yourself. And if you stay in this kind of relationship, you are acknowledging that this kind of abusive energy is what you want in your life.

Remind yourself that real love never makes you feel bad about yourself. Love supports, inspires and allows you to be a better person in its presence than you were without it. If you are holding on to any relationship that is less than what you truly want, that act of holding on may be blocking you from getting the kind of relationship you truly want. If you fill up your life with less than what you want, it is like a cup that is already full; it has no room left to receive anything else. Only when you self-lovingly rid your life of anything that is less than what you want and deserve, will you have room for the very thing you want and desire.

— DIFFERENT FORMS OF LOVE —

One of the greatest vehicles for growth and love is a relationship.

But a relationship doesn't require romance for you to learn from it or receive love from it. One way you may be blocking love from coming into your life is by being attached to the form that it comes in. You can learn from and receive love from all types of people, and you can interact with them on all kinds of levels, not just the romantic level. In our society, we assume that every single man is looking for romance with every single woman and vice versa. The bad part of this is that it discounts all other relationships and puts pressure on men and women to hurriedly move their relationship toward commitment and romance. We believe that many people miss out on a lot of love in their lives because they are not open to all the different forms that love may come in.

Another way you may block love from coming into your life is by presenting yourself as you think others want to see you and not as yourself. This kind of energy says, "I'm not O.K. as I am. I have to be like someone else to be O.K." This energy carries with it a lack of self-love. Over time you will lower your level of self-love, and you will attract less and less love into your life. You will only attract a level of love that exactly matches your own level of love for yourself. And, in this instance, you will attract a relationship that is only interested in the facade you have put on.

Instead, remind yourself that there is no one else in this world exactly like you. Love yourself, not in spite of your differences, but because of them. Your differences are what make you unique. You will be more comfortable and in a lot less pain if you just allow yourself to express and present to the world your natural inclinations and preferences.

Barbara's mom always told her that if she wanted to marry a prince, then she'd have to be a princess. At the time, Barbara didn't realize what wisdom was contained in those words. The truth is that if you want to attract a man or a woman with healthy thinking, then you must also work on your own issues. Working on your own energy is the way to attract a person with a like energy. People who are desperate for love don't feel whole without someone else and, therefore, they will attract a person with the same kind of energy. Being a whole, healthy, self-loving person is the only way to attract a whole, healthy, self-loving person into your life.

ATTRACTING MORE ABUNDANCE
IN YOUR LIFE

*The first thing that needs to be said about abundance is that there
really isn't a good definition of this word. It is like the word success.
You really must form your own definition. We define the word
abundance in the general terms of having more than you need,
or overflowing. This could refer to someone's health, happiness,
or financial situation. Abundance for some people means
having a happy family life, a great job and an ability to pay their bills
every month. Abundance for others has the singular meaning
of total opulence in their lives. Define it for yourself*

because it will help you to attract exactly what it is you want.
For this chapter, however, we will be talking about abundance
in general terms of increasing your financial wealth.

Your ability to attract wealth into your life may have to do with how you see the world in the first place. Notice what your beliefs are about the world. Do you believe in a limited supply of food, money, or anything else we need to exist in this world? Do you believe the only way for you to acquire anything is by taking from others or hurting someone else? Or do you realize that the whole world is made up of the same creative, magnificent energy source whose only limitation is the mind of man?

Think for a moment of how much money there is on this earth. Think about how much money some entrepreneurs, recording artists, actors, corporations, stockbrokers and physicians make in just one year. Now think about all the potential money there is on the earth. Think of the gold, oil, emeralds, diamonds, trees, rich soil, and precious metals that are naturally occurring on this planet. Think of how much of these and other resources there may be out there that we have not yet discovered. The earth is infinitely abundant, and there is more money and potential money on this planet than you can imagine. It may not be in your bank account yet, but the energy of all that money is out there. This planet is so full of incredibly abundant energy that there is enough of everything here to take care of literally everyone. And it is designed so that every person can put out their own energy and get back all that they ever need or want.

There are no limits to the wealth that exists on this planet.

Now may not be the time for everyone on the earth to live abundantly, but that potential is always there. And the potential for you to live in wealth is certainly available for you now, but if you have beliefs within your consciousness about limitation or lack, you will have trouble attracting more wealth into your life. You will need to change those beliefs and change the energy in your consciousness to an energy that matches the vibration of wealth.

— LACK OR ABUNDANCE IN YOUR CONSCIOUSNESS —

One of the first steps to attracting more money into your life is to realize that the amount of money you are now attracting exactly matches the energy that is contained in your consciousness. As you change this energy to align with your natural state of abundance, you will naturally attract more money. We have billions of people living on the earth, some of whom are covering up their pure energy source with their own brand of delusion about themselves and the world. The consciousness of some of them, unfortunately, may hold the energy of poverty. Others have energy that matches gorgeous, opulent homes and large bank accounts. And your energy matches whatever you presently have in your life, but you can change that energy and change your level of abundance.

— ATTITUDE ABOUT PEOPLE WITH MONEY —

Notice what kinds of attitudes you have toward wealthy people or people that you know who increase their wealth. If it makes you jealous for your best friend to get a new car or angry that a stranger lives in a beautiful house, the chances are you have a false belief about lack or limitation. There's also a good chance that you are not really angry at the wealthy stranger, you are angry at yourself for not living in your own natural abundance. You have to want abundance for everyone in order to get it for yourself. And in order to want abundance for everyone, you must believe in an unlimited world and in your own natural abundance.

— GIVING —

Notice your own energy. Do you mostly take or give to others? You limit yourself by always taking because you're probably taking something of far less value than your inner self wants to give to you. The act of taking is an energy that says we live in a limited world where there's not enough for everyone. The energy of taking is about fear and limitation. Taking will only get you lack in return. To stop taking, you may have to be willing to wait to receive something you desire until the time is right and it all falls into place.

Give to others the way you want to be given to. If you hold back with others you'll hold back with yourself. We both tend to give more to the other than to ourselves. And this seems to overflow back to ourselves as we give to each other.

— ABUNDANCE IS YOUR NATURAL STATE —

To increase abundance in your life, you need to realize that abundance is your natural state and to be anything else is unnatural for you. You were created from abundant, infinite, unlimited energy. This energy has never changed. It has only been covered up by false beliefs you have chosen to deposit on top of your core energy. If you look underneath these false beliefs, you will see the truth about yourself. You were born to be an abundant, unlimited being. Your natural state is to live in whatever version of abundance you desire.

Many people have a hard time increasing their financial situation because they don't feel worthy of their natural state of wealth. This is more closely related to self-love issues, and if this seems true for you, make sure to read the chapter about getting more love in your life. A lot of the same concepts and techniques that were covered in that chapter relate here as well. We will cover them in this chapter with an emphasis on how this relates to your abundance.

— GIVE TO YOURSELF —

Unless you can give to yourself, you won't be able to receive the increased wealth you desire. Allow yourself to spend money on yourself for things that you are attracted to. Allow other people to give to you. If the energy of receiving makes you uncomfortable, you will not attract more wealth. Attracting money or wealth has to do with an energy of loving yourself enough to be able to receive the wealth that you want.

— RECEIVING —

Notice whether you are comfortable with others giving to you or waiting on you. If you find that receiving does make you uncomfortable, work on changing that energy in your consciousness. The next time someone offers to give something to you, if only a compliment, receive it graciously. Put yourself in places where you know you will have to let others wait on you. Go to stores where the sales people have to show an item to you. Go out to dinner where a waiter serves you. Treat yourself to a facial or a massage. All of these are services where you will have to receive the energy of another person.

— GET COMFORTABLE WITH WEALTH —

You must feel comfortable with wealth to increase your attraction of it. Allow yourself to go into stores even when you know you don't yet have the money to buy the things sold there. Get the feel of what it's like to be able to buy in those stores. You're not wasting anyone's time because one day you will be able to buy in those stores. Allow the shopkeepers to wait on you and give to you and respond with the confidence of having an unlimited bank account.

This is a good time to practice being the way you will be after you receive your dream. We once bought a compact for Barbara at a very expensive store because she was attracted to it, and we were able to have the experience of shopping and buying something from a luxury store. We also toured a huge, gorgeous home for sale even though we weren't in the market for a new home, just to honor our stirrings that we were both having inside for a nicer home. About a year later our dream home that we now live in popped into our lives when we weren't even looking for a house. Our dream home turned out to be over twice the size of the house we owned then, but it was about the same size as the house we had toured.

— DO ANYTHING THAT MAKES YOU FEEL WEALTHY —

Go places that make you feel wealthy. Wear things that make you feel wealthy. Buy things that make you feel wealthy. Fill your home, your car and your closet with things that make you feel wealthy. The more you align yourself with the energy of wealth, the easier it will be to attract it. We buy a lot of artwork, jewelry and creative decorations for our home that have special meanings of abundance to us. If you can't afford artwork or jewelry yet that has any special abundant meaning for you, try buying something small that you will see every day, like a keychain, which has a symbol representing abundance on it. It doesn't have to be a symbol that represents abundance to everyone else, just to you.

— UPGRADE YOUR LEVEL OF ABUNDANCE EVERY CHANCE YOU GET —

Within the context of taking responsibility for your life, and acting accordingly, allow yourself to upgrade your life whenever you can. However, there must be a responsible balance in giving to yourself versus the irresponsibility of spending beyond your present, physical means. Irresponsibility with money says "I want less of this in my life", and that is exactly what you will get. However, just as spending beyond your means may sabotage your abundance, hoarding your money can too. Hoarding is an energy of fear and of lack. It says "I'm afraid there won't be enough". This kind of energy will attract back a like energy of there not being enough.

— KEEP YOUR ABUNDANCE FLOWING —

Keep your abundance flowing and prepare to receive more

wealth in your life. As you upgrade the abundance level in your life, you can keep your abundance flowing by letting go of the old and making room for the new. This is similar to the analogy we used in the previous chapter about the filled cup not having any room to receive anything else. If you hold on to everything that is presently in your life, and you keep acquiring, pretty soon you won't have room to receive anything new.

The most obvious example of this in our lives is the way we constantly go through our closets and give away clothes that we don't seem to use much anymore. What we find ourselves not wearing anymore we give away. Sometimes a real old friend of a shirt will pull at our heart strings or we'll remember how much we paid for an item or we may notice some attachment to the past or some resistance come up within us. But we let it go anyway, because that is the only way to make room for the beautiful new abundance that we are naturally attracting every moment.

— DON'T BE EMBARRASSED BY WEALTH —

To increase your wealth, you must not be embarrassed by wealth. Notice your feelings when you tell a friend how much you paid for something. Notice if you try to hide how wealthy or abundant you are. Being embarrassed by your wealth says that being wealthy is not your natural state and there is something wrong with being wealthy. If you have people in your life who are not at your level of abundance, the best thing that you can do for them is to continue to be an abundant example for them to show them that living abundantly is possible.

Barbara remembers a co-worker asking about a recent trip to Hawaii, and she was asked how many times she had been there. She reluctantly said five times, knowing that her co-worker had never been. Then she quickly explained that the reason she was able to go so many times was because she had used frequent flyer points to get there. This was not very abundant energy that Barbara put out. She was apologizing for her abundance and making excuses for it. Instead, she could've talked about her trip without apology knowing that her co-worker had the power to increase his abundance and soon could be taking a trip there as well.

— FOCUS YOUR ATTENTION —

Certainly there are plenty of people in the world who attract vast sums of money without focusing on the wealth in their life. But if you look closely there will be some intense focus within those people that at least produces a lot of money as a by-product of that focus. The same techniques that were used in the previous chapter for focusing your attention on love will also work for abundance. Affirmations and visualizations are two of the best.

— NO LIMITS —

Don't limit yourself or your dream. And don't buy into the limits set by society or someone else. If you listen to the negative messages out there, you will soon start to believe them. Create your own positive messages within yourself and they will soon become your reality.

GROUP CONSCIOUSNESS

*Just as each of us has an individual consciousness,
so do we, as members of different groups, have a group consciousness.
Just as the totality of an individual's thoughts, feelings and impressions
make up an individual's consciousness, so does the totality
of a group of people's thoughts, feelings and impressions
make up a group consciousness. So a family has a group consciousness,
and so does a community or a region of this country.
Our nation, or society as we know it, has a group consciousness.
Even corporations and institutions have a group consciousness.
All throughout this book we have talked about the energy of thoughts,
feelings, impressions, and beliefs. As you put people together
in groups (families, companies, communities, nations, etc.),
their collective energies unite to create a collective
or group consciousness.*

The principles of energy which we have talked about in this book relate just as much to group consciousness as they do to individual consciousness. All the principles of energy work the same. Whatever kind of energy we put out as a group will attract back a like energy. The collective group energy attracts people, circumstances and situations that exactly match the group energy.

It's one thing to take responsibility for your own life, but it's really hard to admit that you, your consciousness, your energy, is part of the larger group consciousness. It's tough to admit that each one of us contribute to, say, our nation's consciousness. When you look at the problems in our nation, it may depress you to realize that you are a part of the energy that created those problems. Look at the violence, the prejudice, the hunger, the unhappiness, the diseases and the hatred that exist in our nation. Realize that each of us had a part in creating or allowing it.

One reason we have trouble admitting our responsibility in our nation's group consciousness is because we have, until recently, been a nation asleep. We have allowed the news media and our government to think for us. We have allowed our political system to become bogged down in egos running wild. It's as though we have anesthetized ourselves with the drug of "Let someone else handle it." We have been happy to let our media think for us and our government make decisions for us. That way we didn't have to take a look at ourselves. We didn't have to determine how we really thought or felt. Someone else told us. Someone else failed when it didn't turn out right. We have been happy to throw money at problems instead of getting involved and finding out how we can help our fellow human beings to help themselves.

— VICTIMISM —

We have been happy to sit back and be victims. But along with the victimism that is rampant in our society, comes powerlessness. We have forgotten what a naturally powerful people we are. We have forgotten how naturally loving we are. We have forgotten that we, as powerful and loving beings, can change things for the better.

The good news is, just like we created these problems, we can uncreate them. How, you say? By realizing that each one of us is necessary to make up the group consciousness we can change the world. If you can change your own consciousness concerning violence or prejudice or poverty, then you can change the world.

Think of it this way. The consciousness of the world is presently made up of the sum total of everyone's consciousness, including yours. It is like a kaleidoscope, made up of a myriad of different images, all intricately connected to one another. And the moment you turn the kaleidoscope, everything shifts and becomes an entirely different image.

It's the same way with consciousness, both individual and group. The moment your consciousness changes, you create a shift in the entire group consciousness and it no longer is the same. You have changed the world! In addition, your consciousness, changed back to its natural energy, will be an example for all other people to learn from. Your changed consciousness will be an illustration to others that it is possible to live in love, peace, abundance, fulfillment, intelligence, beauty, fullness, harmony, power, freedom, unlimitedness, excellence and health.

Each one of us is an important and necessary part of the group consciousness. Without any one of us, the group consciousness would be different. Think about it. If you were stranded on a desert island, would you want to be there with only cobblers? Of course not! You would want to have shipbuilders, cooks, engineers, doctors, carpenters, etc. on that island with you. Each person and their unique abilities would be very necessary and very important. If you were stranded on a desert island you would learn to appreciate the differences in each person and what they added to your small society.

But let's face it! We really are stranded on a desert island and that island is named Earth. Just because our society is larger doesn't mean that each person who makes up our society isn't just as important and necessary as they would be with a smaller scale society. So let's learn to embrace our differences and by doing so we will change the love consciousness of the world.

— CHANGE THE WAY YOU SEE
THE DIFFERENCES IN OTHERS —

If you think about it, the Universe could have expressed Itself in the dark. Our planet could have been created in total darkness, without a sun or a moon. Think how much we would have missed visually if this had happened. We would not have been able to see the variety of leaves, the myriad of greens, the colors of fish or the glorious sunsets. But we also wouldn't have been able to see the physical differences in our own species. We would only be able to know one another by our spirits, not by our physical features. The Universe didn't create it that way. The Universe created our world with light. The light was given to us so that we can see the differences, not in order to judge them, but to delight in them and appreciate them. Each of us is unique, necessary and beautiful. Change the world by changing the way you see the differences in others.

— PUT YOUR MONEY WHERE YOUR CONSCIOUSNESS IS —

Another way to change the world is to change your actions. Don't watch television that tries to think for you. Don't vote for politicians that serve themselves instead of you. Vote for people that represent the kind of energy that you feel is most like your own energy. Put your money where your consciousness is. Money is a powerful tool when put in the hands of group consciousness. Spend your money on products that advertise on uplifting, positive, television shows.

Buy magazines that write articles that empower people rather than turn them into sleeping clones.

Don't be fooled into thinking that you couldn't possibly harm or change the world by the energy you put out. Many people cheat on government programs, shoplift from stores or trade illegal stock tips. They think no one is hurt by this energy. They're wrong. We all feel the effects of this energy and therefore people who cheat large institutions are really hurting themselves. And, of course, we all feel the physical consequences of increased prices and bigger budget deficits. If just one person stops shoplifting and changes their consciousness towards their natural abundance, the world is a changed place.

— THERE IS ALWAYS HOPE —

Remember, there is always hope for everyone. Everyone on the planet can change their consciousness. Remember too that we live in an unlimited universe. And we are unlimited people. Think for yourself. Be aware. Change the world.

ABOUT THE AUTHORS

Barbara and Jimmie Lewis are co-authors of two books, *The Energy of Life* and *The Real Miracle*. They wrote each book as a way of solidifying what they were learning about life and as a way of sharing what they learned with the rest of the world.

Barbara and Jimmie helped each other learn about the energy of life from the Spring of 1988 until the Spring of 2002 when they learned that miraculous living was an inside job. They went through a life-changing process that stripped away all of their worldly security and caused them to rely only on their inner being and discovered the real miracle within. *The Real Miracle* is an intimate revelation of their experience through this process and contains nuggets of truth that can be used by anyone.

When Barbara and Jimmie got together as a couple in 1988 they knew instantly that their relationship was to be a vehicle for spiritual awakening. They went to graduate school together and became counseling psychologists with a double major in transpersonal psychology and relationships in order to learn everything they could about relationships and spiritual awakening. As licensed psychotherapists they specialized in relationships.

When Barbara and Jimmie manifested their vision of living in financial and time freedom they moved from busy lives in Houston to a mountain retreat in Northern California on December 10, 2008. Their remaining time together, and how they used their relationship for spiritual awakening, is beautifully expressed in Jimmie's moving account of their lives in his third book, *A Holy Relationship: The Memoir of One Couple's Transformation.*

Barbara left the physical on August 31, 2010.

For personal appearances, workshops, retreats, group or private sessions:
jimmie@jimmielewis.com
www.jimmielewis.com

CPSIA information can be obtained at www.ICGtesting.com
Printed in the USA
LVOW07s0104081015

457425LV00036B/403/P

9 780991 462926